**Books are to be returned on or before
the last date below.**

Governance and Risk in Emerging and Global Markets

Centre for the Study of Emerging Markets Series

Series Editor: **Dr Sima Motamen-Samadian**

The Centre for the Study of Emerging Markets (CSEM) Series provides a forum for assessing various aspects of emerging markets. The series includes the latest theoretical and empirical studies from both academics and practitioners in relation to the economies and financial markets of emerging markets. These cover a wide range of subjects, including stock markets and their efficiency in emerging markets, forecasting models and their level of accuracy in emerging markets, dynamic models and their application in emerging markets, sovereign debt and its implications, exchange rate regimes and their merits, risk management in emerging markets, derivative markets and hedging decisions in emerging markets, and governance and risk in emerging markets.

The series will be one of the main sources of reference on emerging markets, both within and outside those markets, for academics, national and international agencies, and financial institutions.

Titles include:

Sima Motamen-Samadian (*editor*)
DYNAMIC MODELS AND THEIR APPLICATIONS IN EMERGING MARKETS

CAPITAL FLOWS AND FOREIGN DIRECT INVESTMENTS IN EMERGING MARKETS

RISK MANAGEMENT IN EMERGING MARKETS

GOVERNANCE AND RISK IN EMERGING AND GLOBAL MARKETS

Also by Sima Motamen-Samadian

INTERNATIONAL DEBT AND CENTRAL BANKING IN THE 1980s
(*edited with Z. Res*)

EMERGING MARKETS
Past and Present Experiences, and Future Prospects (*edited with C. Garido*)

Centre for the Study of Emerging Markets Series
Series Standing Order ISBN 1–4039–9521–4

You can receive future titles in this series as they are published by placing a standing order. Please contact your bookseller or, in case of difficulty, write to us at the address below with your name and address, the title of the series and one of the ISBNs quoted above.

Customer Services Department, Macmillan Distribution Ltd, Houndmills, Basingstoke, Hampshire RG21 6XS, England

---

Governance and Risk in Emerging and Global Markets

Edited by

Sima Motamen-Samadian

First published in 2005 by
PALGRAVE MACMILLAN
Houndmills, Basingstoke, Hampshire RG21 6XS and
175 Fifth Avenue, New York, N.Y. 10010
Companies and representatives throughout the world.

PALGRAVE MACMILLAN is the global academic imprint of the Palgrave
Macmillan division of St. Martin's Press, LLC and of Palgrave Macmillan
Ltd. Macmillan® is a registered trademark in the United States, United
Kingdom and other countries. Palgrave is a registered trademark in the
European Union and other countries.

ISBN-13: 978–1–4039–9156–0
ISBN-10: 1–4039–9156–1

This book is printed on paper suitable for recycling and made from fully
managed and sustained forest sources.

A catalogue record for this book is available from the British Library.

Library of Congress Cataloging-in-Publication Data
    Governance and risk in emerging and global markets / edited by
Sima Motamen-Samadian.
        p. cm.—(Centre for the Study of Emerging Markets series)
    Includes bibliographical references and index.
    ISBN 1–4039–9156–1 (cloth)
    1. Investments – Developing countries. 2. Securities – Developing
countries. 3. Credit – Developing countries. 4. Risk management –
Developing countries. 5. Developing countries – Economic policy.
    I. Motamen-Samadian, Sima. II. Series.
HG5993.G68 2005
332.6′09172′4—dc22   2005047133

10 9 8 7 6 5 4 3 2 1
14 13 12 11 10 09 08 07 06 05

Printed and bound in Great Britain by
Antony Rowe Ltd, Chippenham and Eastbourne

Contents

List of Figures and Tables

Figures

Preface

The eight studies presented in this volume are put together to provide a new insight into the issue of governance and risk management in emerging and global markets. The objective is to identify some of the factors that can affect governance, and some of the measures that public authorities and managers of companies might adopt to reduce risks of failure. The chapters provide a theoretical and empirical analysis of governance, regulatory failure, country risk analysis, and risk management in emerging and developed countries. The topics discussed are important and useful for all those who consider operating or investing in emerging and non-emerging markets. Chapter 1 is the introduction; Chapter 2 provides a critical discussion of the Basel II Capital Accord and the possibility of regulatory failure; Chapter 3 is based on some empirical studies on UK firms and presents a new technique of early-warning credit signal that can detect risks of default. Chapter 4 uses a risk analysis to identify the most appropriate production system in Pakistan's agricultural sector. Chapter 5 tries to establish whether official and private creditors take issues related to governance and corruption into consideration when they assess country risk. Chapter 6 examines the extent by which stockmarket liberalizations in emerging markets can transmit the volatility of those markets to other international markets such as the United States and Japan, while in Chapter 7 the authors focus on Iraq's stockmarket, and provide an assessment of its past performance and future prospects. Finally, Chapter 8 provides a discussion of the enormous costs of reconstruction of Iraq, and proposes securitization of the country's assets as a means to cover those substantial costs.

SIMA MOTAMEN-SAMADIAN

Acknowledgements

This volume is a collection of some of the papers presented at the International Conference on Emerging Markets and Global Risk Management in June 2004 in London. The conference was organized by the Centre for the Study of Emerging Markets (CSEM) at the Westminster Business School. In this respect my sincere thanks go to Hanna Scobie at the European Economic and Financial Centre who inspired and supported me in organizing the conference.

My special thanks go to all the contributors for their timely delivery of the chapters and to my family and in particular my husband Vahab Samadian for his continuous support through the period when I was working on the book.

SIMA MOTAMEN-SAMADIAN

Notes on the Contributors

Michel H. Bouchet is Professor of Finance, Global Finance Chair, at the CERAM Sophia Antipolis, France.

Bertrand Groslambert is Professor of Finance at the CERAM Sophia Antipolis, France.

Maqsood Hussain is Assistant Professor in Economics at the Department of Agricultural Economics, University of Agriculture, Faisalabad, Pakistan.

Talal Kadhim is a Senior Lecturer in Quantitative Methods at the Westminster Business School, University of Westminster, United Kingdom.

Sima Motamen-Samadian is Director of the Centre for the Study of Emerging Markets and a Principal Lecturer in Economics at the Westminster Business School, University of Westminster, United Kingdom.

Duc Nguyen is a Researcher in Finance at the University of Grenoble II, France.

Ann Puri is a Senior Lecturer in Quantitative Methods at the Westminster Business School, University of Westminster, United Kingdom.

Abdul Saboor is Assistant Professor in Economics at the Department of Agricultural Economics, University of Agriculture, Faisalabad, Pakistan.

Ola Sholarin is a Lecturer in Economics and Quantitative Methods at the Westminster Business School, University of Westminster, United Kingdom.

Kadom Shubber is a Senior Lecturer in Finance at the Westminster Business School, University of Westminster, United Kingdom.

Joseph Tanega is a Senior Lecturer in Business Law at the Westminster Business School, University of Westminster, United Kingdom.

Harry Thapar is a Senior Lecturer in Business Law at the Westminster Business School, University of Westminster, United Kingdom.

1
Introduction

Sima Motamen-Samadian

Introduction

In recent years, the failure of a number of large corporations and sovereign states to meet their obligations has highlighted the crucial role of governance in risk management. It has become evident that while good governance at both the micro and macro levels can enhance the opportunities of firms, industries and countries, poor governance can have devastating effects on a wider community.

Following each financial crisis, or revelation of a mega company failure, researchers have gone into a frenzy of study to understand the sources of risks and the causes of failure. At the same time, national and international agencies have tried to revise the existing rules and introduce new regulations that can reduce the risks of corporate failure in both financial and non-financial markets.

The new rules are usually designed to limit the scope of poor governance, and reduce the adverse side-effects of corporate failure on the rest of the economy, or for that matter the global economy. Nevertheless, despite the continuous revision of existing practices, the introduction of new rules and regulations, and the adoption of varied methods of risk management, there remain a number of other variables that require consideration.

The array of variables that can influence governance at both corporate and country level are numerous. Some of these are at the firm level such as the adoption of a particular method of operation, or a specific method of risk evaluation, and some are at country level such as the introduction of a new regulatory environment that might affect the operation of individual firms or a market within an economy or within global markets.

The objective of this book is threefold. First, it tries to demonstrate some of the factors that can shape or influence governance in different types of activities. Second, it tries to shed some light on some of the methods that firms can adopt in their activities to reduce and manage risks in both emerging and non-emerging markets; methods that can enhance the quality of governance and reduce risks of operation failure and default. Third, it draws attention to some of the needs of totally new markets and the importance of sound governance in their future survival.

Chapter 2 explains how new regulations might affect the governance of institutions that operate under the new regulatory environment. Here Tanaga tries to widen and deepen the perspectives on the Basel II implementation, and demonstrates the possibility of regulatory failure. In his assessment, although the rules of the Basel II Capital Accord were initially designed to reduce systemic risk, there are a number of potential unintended consequences that might arise from its operating principles and attempted implementation in practice. Some of these unintended consequences can be viewed as outcomes of moral hazard and adverse selection. Tanaga highlights the dangers of setting risk-based rules, which can incentivize risk-takers to exploit the rules and consider strategies that tread the fine line between regulatory avoidance and regulatory evasion. In his exposition, Tanaga sets out the fundamental principles of avoiding regulatory failure, and provides critical tools of assessment and evaluation to policy-makers and supervisory authorities for the successful implementation of the Basel II principles.

Chapter 3 shows how governance can be improved if managers employ a new technique of early-warning credit signals that can detect the risks of default. Here Puri and Thapar, based on an examination of a wide range of companies, propose a hypothetical model that provides a better understanding of the default process in selected UK sectors. In their study of the default process, they identify a number of disparate and unrelated value-destructive factors that adversely affect the position of the company over time. In the first stage these factors tend to limit the company's growth opportunities, while in the second stage they tend to consolidate and erode any further growth possibilities, and over a longer period they conspire to destroy shareholder value, before finally leading to the total failure of a firm. The early-warning credit signal model presented here can assist managers to understand the role of destructive factors and reverse a firm's decline. The level of intervention and costs involved would depend on the timing and extent of the remedial action taken by the management of a company. In their study the authors have considered the position of a number of companies in three UK sectors – telecommunications, utilities, and the retail sector – and tried to utilize a company risk measurement method, based on a single-index market model. The company risk measure mapped well onto Moody's KMV expected default frequency (EDF) credit-risk measure. Results revealed that the naïve model had sufficient discriminatory power to pick up credit-related changes, and the technique was considered to be particularly useful as an internal metric for a corporate risk manager.

Chapter 4 focuses more on risk management and looks at a more appropriate method of production in Pakistan's agricultural sector that can reduce risks of crop failure. Here, Hussain and Saboor highlight the importance of the agricultural sector in Pakistan's economy where it accounts for 24 per cent of the GDP and employs 48.4 per cent of the total workforce. They point out how agricultural producers are faced with both risk and uncertainty and how the combination of the two can influence the efficiency of resource-use in agricultural decision-making processes. The low elasticities of prices and incomes in this sector, in the presence of risk and uncertainty, can lead to wide swings in crop prices and severely test farmers' risk-bearing capacities. In this respect the production system adopted by farmers can have important implications on their future survival. Therefore, if farmers' risk-bearing capacities can be evaluated before the risks take effect, they can take precautionary measures to increase their marginal profit. To assess this risk-bearing capacity, Hussain and Saboor consider two production systems, namely Zero Tillage (ZT), which is a sustainable crop production system that conserves the soil as well as resources, and Conventional Tillage (CT) which leads to soil deterioration and is a non-sustainable crop-production system. Their study reveals that the former is a preferred system of production to the latter. They also show that not only does ZT conserve the soil water, it also reduces the cost of production and requires very little initial investment cost.

In Chapter 5, Bouchet and Groslambert try to establish whether official and private creditors who are assessing country risk take issues related to governance and corruption into consideration. They point out that investors and creditors look for an optimal combination of robust fundamentals, socio-political stability and government efficiency. Therefore, the quality of governance should play a very important role in their decision-making. In practice, however, when looking at actual risk exposure by private capital markets and official institutions, one cannot find much evidence of a relationship between corruption and lending flows. Bouchet and Groslambert show that, at best, corruption is not a driving element of lending decisions, and at worst some creditors seem to back corrupt governments. In their view, much remains to be done to reconcile governance, country risk assessment and strategy decision-making.

In Chapter 6, Nguyen provides an empirical analysis of market deregulation and its role in volatility spillover. Here the author examines the extent by which stockmarket liberalizations in emerging markets can transmit the volatility of those markets to other international markets such as the United States and Japan. Nguyen's results reinforce previous findings in that emerging markets tend to generate higher volatility than developed markets. Other studies in the past have often suggested that sudden changes in emerging market volatility were associated with financial liberalizations. Nguyen's tests of the relationship between financial liberalization and volatility, however, reveal conflicting results about the sign of financial liberalization effects. He also finds that stock volatility is substantially transmitted among sample markets, especially between emerging markets of the same geographical location. According to his results, the multilateral transmission of volatility only increases slightly after liberalization programmes. Finally, he argues that shocks to volatility in emerging markets, as opposed to the US and Japanese markets, are the main factors that constitute a dominant source of return variability in foreign stockmarkets.

In Chapter 7, governance is examined at the market and country levels. Here Shubber and Kadhim examine the growth of Iraq's stockmarket over the last decade, and highlight its specific features and prospects for development. The authors explain how asset price movements on the Baghdad bourse were dominated by international events rather than corporate news, and how the market was characterized by a small number of Iraqi firms and low capitalization. The authors describe how the market restarted its operations in 2003, and discuss how it may play a pivotal role in Iraq's economic development, provided the authorities adopt liberal policies towards incoming investment from neighbouring countries, the Iraqi expatriate community and Western investors. In the authors' view, any concrete schemes for increased regional cooperation can boost the revamped exchange. Thus this chapter highlights the importance of governance at country level for the growth of a financial market.

Finally, in Chapter 8 Sholarin examines the prospect of securitization of Iraqi assets and the associated risks for the country. The author discusses the need for financial resources to rebuild the economy and country, pointing out that although Iraq has oil and gas resources that can help in financing the cost of reconstruction, they cannot be relied upon solely. The magnitude of the financial resources required for reconstruction are likely to be far greater than the proceeds of oil and gas exports. Therefore, to cover the cost of reconstruction, Sholarin proposes a whole range of securitization of Iraqi assets. The success of such a programme, however, would depend on a number of economic, political and regulatory preconditions that should be met, all of which, ultimately, depend on the nature and style of governance to be adopted by the official agencies in Iraq.

Overall, this book provides an interesting range of discussions on various forms of governance at different levels in emerging and non-emerging markets.

2

Basel II: Principles of Avoiding Regulatory Failure

Joseph Tanega *

Introduction

In this chapter I focus on the risk of regulatory failure in implementing the new Basel II requirements. It would be fair to say that whilst the intention of Basel II is to detect, manage and control the risk of capital inadequacy at the individual bank level, a large uncertainty looms over its successful implementation on a global basis. I shall draw attention to a range of possible unintended effects, to anticipate solutions which may be implemented by a variety of small and medium-sized financial institutions, especially in the emerging markets. The chapter is divided into three main sections: the private and public justification of the Basel II design; a theoretical model of regulatory design; and the major types of regulatory failure.

We begin our analysis with an examination of the private and public justification of Basel II, which broadly defines the scope of solutions for micro-economic and macro-economic policy formulation. We next present a theoretical model of regulatory design that takes into account the critical risk path that financial institutions face in implementing Basel II standards. In the third part we present five major types of regulatory failure pertinent to Basel II, and suggest potential solutions which may be implemented at both the country supervisory level, and at the individual financial institution level. Our overall conclusion, however, is not optimistic since there are

* I would like to thank Tamara Machavariani for her research assistance in the completion of this work.

inherent design ambiguities of Basel II which are yet to be resolved, and a number of issues concerning fairness of implementation which are already being challenged across a broad and highly polarized field of financial institutions. We ask whether Basel II as a regulatory instrument would enable regulators to anticipatorily detect individual bank failure. The positive answer to this question is subject to a number of conditions, which we label as the top-five risks to the successful implementation of Basel II. Seen from another perspective, these risks also define a critical path in which each risk can be viewed as a potential failure node. This chapter is intended as a contribution towards understanding what real hurdles need to be overcome for Basel II to progress towards an optimum model of regulatory control in the global banking system.

Private and public justification of the Basel II design

The private justification for the Basel II design

The private justification for Basel II is that it enables banks and other financial institutions to be regulated according to a set of regulatory standards, supervisory review and disclosures which closely mirrors the practical types of information which management needs in order to manage and control its risks in a well-run and ongoing basis. As such, Basel II forms a market signal of how modern banks should be managed and controlled.

Evidence of this view comes from the recent papers of the Basel Banking Committee embracing the concept of economic capital as a general methodology for risk aggregation.[1] The challenge of risk aggregation is to compute all the various forms of risk that a bank might face under one common measurement. Despite its limited classification of risk categories, Basel II signals a radical shift in banking regulations bringing them into line with the intellectual scientific spirit of the post-Newtonian age. In the pre-Newtonian age, real quantities were the undeniable sense perceptions caused by physical quantities – such as the physical quantity of money and their equivalent demarcations in double-entry accounting systems. In the post-Newtonian world, the scientist was concerned with rules that allowed for a simplification of calculating the interaction of a system of objects. These rules were based on seeing the 'change of change', (that is the acceleration) that allowed us to view a large range of physical phenomena in terms of algorithmic operations. One of the major points of Basel II is that it forces banking regulators to consciously conceive of risk in terms of not just the negative quality of loss and liability, but as change in the sense of volatility.

Along this same line of thought, we see that setting the appropriate range of values for capital at risk is the essence of 'economic-capital' methodologies which are aimed at providing a common set of metrics for quantifying risk across a diverse range of events, at the same time allowing for the calculation of the amount of capital that a bank should hold to support the various levels of risk-taking.[2] Whilst we need not examine the large number of definitions of economic capital in the literature,[3] it is important to see how closely aligned the Basel II requirements are to risk categories, which are in use for managing financial institutions.

From the perspective of managers in financial institutions, the major risk that needs to be managed and controlled is the volatility of earnings (see Figure 2.1). There are many ways we can decompose this risk, and for our purposes the first distinction is between financial risk and non-financial risk. The financial risks are those taken by the financial institution as a financial intermediary or as owner of financial products. Financial risks can be further decomposed into the well-known risk types of credit risk and market risk, as well as managing

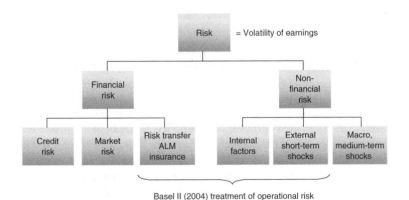

Figure 2.1 Basel II in terms of financial and non-financial risks

asset-liability risk, underwriting risk, insurance and a whole host of derivatives risk, involving new instruments such as credit derivatives, credit default swaps and warrant bonds. What distinguishes the business of a financial institution from other types of business is its financial products.

As we can see from Figure 2.1, if we consider that credit risk and market risk are covered in the normal sense under Basel II, and that insurance, internal factors and external short-term shocks are covered under the definition of Basel II for operational risk, then Basel II covers a great portion of the financial and non-financial risk envelope.

The non-financial risks, however, are not unique to the financial industry but are instead the functions and processes that are in common with most other businesses. We decompose non-financial risks into 'internal factors', 'external short-term shocks' and 'macro medium-term shocks'. The definition of operational risk in Basel II includes exposure to failure concerning people, processes, systems, technology and external events. These are covered by the 'internal factors' and 'external short-term shocks'. Recently, Basel II has incorporated insurance into the calculation of operational risk capital.[4] Basel II now allows a deduction of the total notional amount of insurance coverage up to 80 per cent of the capital required under the Advanced Measurement Approach (AMA) of operational risk. For example, if the total amount of operational risk capital required under the AMA of Basel II is £200 million, and if the bank were to purchase insurance with a notional amount of £100 million, it would be able to deduct only down to the floor of 80 per cent of £200 million (that is, £160 million).

The question is whether Basel II is poised to cover an even larger portion of the entire non-financial risk area. It is possible that it might be developed in that direction, but currently operational risk under Basel II specifically excludes 'strategic and reputational risks'.[5] However, it may be the case that regulators may need to examine these types of risks as part of their risk review of the banking processes. For example, under the so-called 'ARROW Risk Review' of the UK Financial Services Authority (UK FSA), the regulator may examine 45 risk types, including 'strategic business risks'.[6] However, it is difficult to see how a regulatory authority in areas such as 'medium-term shocks', for example the effects of terrorist attacks on medium-term profitability, could be or should be controlled by regulatory action.

Indeed, using the model in Figure 2.1 where earnings volatility is simply a combination of financial risk and non-financial risk, it becomes obvious that deducting financial risk from earnings volatility should give an indication of the quantum of non-financial risks. And, carrying this method further, if we could but have a better estimation of credit risk, market risk, risk transfers, internal factors and external short-term shocks, we would be able to deduce the value of external medium-term shocks. But this could happen only in an imaginary perfect world of complete markets, perfect information, and naïve anti-Machiavellian competitors! In the practical world of banking, in its cut and thrust of new product innovations and the violent movements of asset prices around liquidity black holes and irrational exuberance, the science and art of estimating appropriate capital is more art than science. A more realistic justification for Basel II's existence comes from the undeniable hard facts of history – bank failures.

The public justification: to protect against potential bank failures

Whilst Basel II does not appear to have an explicit statement to the effect that the regulatory capital requirement is to protect against bank failures, it may be reasonable to pose the simple question given the quantum of effort required to fully comply with Basel II: 'Is Basel II designed to prevent bank failures?'

To banking professionals, the minimum capital requirements of Basel II are so obviously related to preventing bank failures that nothing more needs to be stated. It is a matter of financial doctrine that without a minimum capital requirement more banks would fail. The retort is that the minimum regulatory capital requirement should always be less than what a prudent bank would hold in any case. To put this point more bluntly, on the one hand, if Basel II is not aimed at preventing bank failures then the entire regulatory intent to establish Basel II is misconceived. On the other hand, if Basel II is designed to prevent bank failures, we might ask whether the design features and changes that Basel II advocates are reasonably related to meeting this goal. To this end a theoretical model of regulatory design will be described that may be used for the purpose of critical risk management in financial institutions. I hope this model may throw light on the micro-prudential and macro-prudential objectives of financial regulation.[7] In another paper I examine the public justification of Basel II in light of the Basel Committee's research on bank failures,[8] but in this chapter I focus on four fundamental principles of regulatory design and the critical risk path for successful implementation.

Theoretical constraints on regulatory design

A natural way to explain a theoretical model of regulatory design is to start with a sketch of unobjectionable first principles and build up the resolving the power of those principles as we examine the details of the regulatory regime. The gist of the first principles remains, but the application of the principles in particular instances will require layers of interpretation which will no doubt engender debate and further resolution.

In this section I put forward a fundamental analysis of regulatory design aimed at helping us understand the critical characteristics for the successful implementation of risk-based regulations such as Basel II. We posit four general constraints for the optimum design of any risk-based regulation. These constraints are based on the principles of a legal contract where the most important features include mutual assent, certainty and exchange of risk and return. Contracts allow individuals to parse uncertainty into tradable (or exchangeable) financial economic units. Simply put, we assume an initial symmetric relationship between regulator and regulatee, and that these four constraints enable a third party to judge whether such a relationship remains in a dynamic symmetry, or verges towards an asymmetry in favour of one or the other parties. Whilst a dynamic asymmetric relationship is possible for the short term, it is assumed that such asymmetry is not sustainable without deception over any period of time since such a relationship would strongly violate a principle of equivalence, or as Rawls puts it, the Second Principle of Justice.[9] The four constraints are as follows:

- Avoid moral hazard
- Avoid adverse selection
- Enhance certainty
- Aim for stability

and we briefly define each constraint in turn.

Avoid moral hazard

This means that the design of the regulatory regime should be such that the explicit incentive-based system of the regulation does not establish perverse incentives which would defeat the purpose of the regulation. For example, under Basel II the explicit incentive of advanced approaches to risk management is the reduction of the regulatory capital risk charge. Since the advanced approaches could conceivably reduce the amount of capital, there is a danger that Basel II might actually provide incentives to export capital outside the banking system. The opportunity for moral hazard is even greater where, in the Basel II case for advanced approaches, the regulator simply approves the bank's sophisticated risk model without direct testing of its accuracy. Given the limited resources of regulators, one wonders who will pay to have competent experts scrutinize the internal workings of advanced risk models. The market asymmetry for this expertise is evident in the large difference in remuneration between top quantitative analysts in large banks and regulators. Thus, unless regulators can pay for this competence, it is unlikely that they will have the requisite ability and resources to independently judge whether advanced risk models are appropriately calibrated. In this case, the risk of moral hazard and regulatory capture would be severe.

Avoid adverse selection

Adverse selection can be defined as a system of rules which, taken together, have the effect of encouraging the worst risk-takers to self-select and to grow in size and number. As this segment of the population is encouraged to grow by virtue of the operation of the regulation which was originally intended to eliminate or reduce the characteristics of this population, the purpose of the regulation is defeated by its operation. Basel II does not appear at first glance to have any considerable adverse selection problem, although the bipolar division between basic or standard approaches and advanced approaches means that less-sophisticated risk-takers are at a competitive disadvantage under the Basel II rules. They are at a competitive disadvantage because they are not able to partake of the diversification and netting benefits of the sophisticated approaches, and because they will not therefore enjoy the benefits of potential reductions in regulatory required capital. As a result, these banks may have the incentive to take on more risks which may not be sufficiently covered by the more basic approaches to calculating credit, market and operational risks. As more banks self-select to opt for more basic approaches, more risk enters the banking system, with a heightened potential for a greater number of bank failures.

Enhance certainty

Regulations can be legally struck down if they are too vague to be enforced or too arbitrary and capricious to be fair. One of the major problems with Basel II is that until we gain more experience in finding common interpretations of risk types, in identifying and measuring relevant and material operational risks, and in calibrating risks relative to changes in equity value, Basel II runs the risk of alienating the banking community. Enhancement and clarity of fundamental principles are far more important than ticking the thousands of reporting details which have little or no relation to the real risks of the business of banking. Clarity of principle, not in amassing details, is required for legislation to be sustainable.

Aim for stability

A risk-based regulatory regime, at least theoretically, should be able to better control the outputs of the regulated system since the regulatory regime should have relatively more sensitive and accurate means of risk-detection. Basel II enables regulators to detect market signals through reports on regulatory capital, inspections and disclosures on a range of risk types.

With the great number of substantive outcomes which are required to be produced as information outputs and the qualitative assessments which the regulator must conduct, the challenge of writing a simple algorithm which captures all possible interactions of regulatory intervention appears at first sight to be insurmountable. However, the four design constraints above may also act as criteria for determining whether particular regulatory actions are rationally related to the overall regulatory objective. These design criteria can be applied more generally to the implementation process of any risk-based regulatory regime. To turn the tables, the Basel II implementation process poses not only a regulatory burden risk to firms, but also of regulatory risk failure to the regulators themselves. We turn now to see how these design constraints may help us understand the logical framework of risk-based regulations.

Risk management for the regulator

To sharpen the discussion about Basel II implementation risk, we will use the actuarial curve as a qualitative model of the regulator's risk profile in implementing Basel II (see Figure 2.2). The four design constraints outlined above may be used to help guide the construction of policies which would reduce the risk of regulatory failure. If for example a proposed policy were to increase moral hazard, adverse selection, uncertainty or instability in the financial system, then such a policy should be rejected. If any of these design constraints were to be violated then the risk of regulatory failure increases, with greater litigation contesting the legality of the legislation, escalating to changes in political authority, to covert and overt defiance of the laws and, finally, total rejection of the law by society. We highlight these risks in more detail below.

The first part of the curve in Figure 2.2 indicates expected losses, or business as usual losses that are anticipated in the ordinary course of business. For regulators, this would mean prosecutorial costs, staff

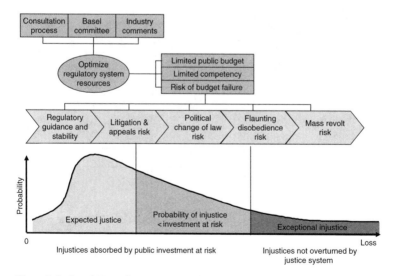

Figure 2.2   Basel II implementation risk curve

turnover costs, computer breakdowns, and anything else likely to be foreseen in the budgeting process and in the ordinary course of a regulator's activities. If a loss is expected, then it is something that can be covered within the regulator's budget. *Pari passu*, an expected loss for a private company should be covered by its profit margin in the sale of its products and services.

The unexpected loss section of the curve describes losses which are not anticipated by the normal activities of the business. For regulators, this might include sudden changes in political parties, new case law that needs to be implemented, or government officials colluding with banks to defraud the government.

Finally, there is the exceptional loss portion of the curve, which defines events that would be uneconomical for the corporate entity to fund through profit margins, reserves or provisions. Here the event has an extreme impact on the business, causing business interruption, and out of this abnormal operating position, where the company is in effect paralyzed, its resuscitation will depend on the amount of risk transfer capital it has been able to purchase and eventually utilize.

Using the same risk typology and applying it to Basel II (see Figure 2.3), we see that the normal or expected loss risk part of the

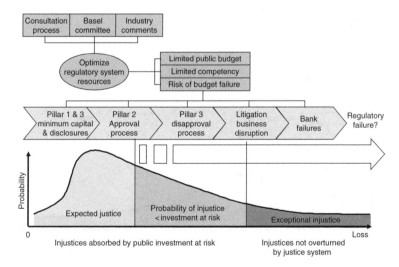

Figure 2.3   Regulatory intensity

curve roughly corresponds to the regular reporting of regulatory capital under Pillar One (which sets out the regulators' capital calculations) and other risk disclosures under Pillar three (which sets out the required disclosures). In this business-as-usual part of the curve, the Pillar Two supervisory review process will be conducted. If all goes well, then regulatory approval will be given and we reach the limit of expected losses.

If the Pillar Two approval process is very involved, resource-intensive and time-consuming for both regulator and regulatee, then there is a higher risk that unexpected risk may occur, including regulatory amplification of the bank's expected risks. If the Pillar Two process ends in disapproval by the regulator then we may encounter a strong counter-reaction by the protesting bank. Banks are not only prone to use litigation, they are also powerful political agents that frequently lobby for change of legislation, change of political parties and deposal of politically appointed officials. If the bank decides to 'up the ante' then the regulatory intensity also increases and the resolution is unlikely to be mutually beneficial and the conflict resolution may be laborious, distractive and very costly to both disputants. The time spent in litigation, the distraction in management time, and the high transaction costs in finding a 'just solution', results in layers of capital being transferred to the legal profession. This would certainly be a grave unintended consequence of Basel II. Given the risks of regulatory failure, it is important for regulators to consider how rising regulatory intensity may be avoided, or at least reasonably reduced.

Critical risk management

Having outlined both the general constraints for regulatory design and a general risk model for the qualitative risk categorization of major components of Basel II, we are still lacking a model for how regulators may implement regulations in terms of their particular decisions. It is at the level of decision-making where we may have perfectly clear regulatory definitions implemented badly, or even vague definitions implemented in an appropriate and efficient manner. Although the types of decision-making may implicate a large body of interpretative theory, we consider decisions in terms of a communications systems framework as in Figure 2.4.

Under this general model, it is assumed that the regulator has ideal goals and that these ideal goals are too vague to be actually physically

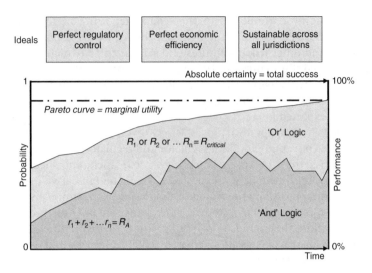

Figure 2.4   Critical risk management model

achievable. Therefore, they lie beyond the boundary of certainty and 100 per cent performance. These ideals may be simple mission statements such as 'perfect regulatory control', 'perfect economic efficiency' or a regulatory regime that is 'sustainable across all jurisdictions'.

Regulatory performance in relation to these ideal goals can be described in terms of two types of logical statements. The first type consists of 'and-logic' statements, which taken together form a volatile level of performance. In Figure 2.4 the volatile performance level is defined by $r_1 + r_2 + r_3 \ldots r_n = R_A$. Decisions made under an 'and-logic' mode are good for generating a wide range of alternatives for testing hypotheses, but the lessons learned are limited by the process of taking even more 'and-logic' type decisions. The major characteristic of the set of and-logic statements is that eliminating one decision-statement at a time does not catastrophically destroy the performance level of the entire set of and-logic decisions.

The second type of decisions consists of 'or-logic' statements, which form a critical path. This means that each decision is critical to the success of the whole series of or-logic statements. If even one or-logic statement is eliminated from the set of or-logic statements, then the entire performance level falls catastrophically.

Most human communities and communication systems are composed of a combination of both types of decision statements. In theory, at some point the cost of eliminating error is more expensive that the gain – the so-called Pareto optimality.[10] However, before that limit on efficiency is ever reached, decisions made within an organization can be modelled as a non-optimum combination of both types of logical statements. The logical and practical consequence of this model is that we can improve the performance of a group of decision-makers if we can help them find the critical path and have them commit and utilize resources to ensure that none of the steps (so-called 'failure nodes') in the critical path are susceptible to catastrophic error.

Given Basel II's complexity and consequent large costs of compliance costs, there are a number of risks of regulatory failure which hang in the balance and must be considered over the course of the proposed implementation period from 2004 to 2006 for the more foundational approaches, and to the end of 2007 for the more sophisticated approaches. We offer the following analysis of *critical failure points* as a means of helping regulators avoid or reduce their risk exposures to successfully implementing the Basel II operating principles.

Avoiding regulatory failure

The Economist defines regulatory failure as 'regulation [which] generates more costs than benefits'.[11] Whilst a purely economic analysis of Basel II may indicate whether it is economically viable, this would only indicate its viability in terms of efficient procedure, which is a species of 'procedural justice', and not whether it is inherently just or fair, which would be considered 'substantive justice'. Basel II's lofty implied goal is to reduce global systemic risk, and its methods for accomplishing this goal are enshrined in specific and detailed operational procedures. Thus, on the one hand, the outstanding goal of Basel II may be substantively just in that all parties affected by its ambit would prefer to live under its bounds than without them, and, on the other hand, Basel II's specific set of rules may lead to a number of unintended consequences and potential regulatory failures. In our analysis, it is important to keep in mind the four design constraints concerning moral hazard, adverse selection, certainty and stability and the distinction between and-logic and or-logic since these constraints act as thematic issues which arise in various guises and combinations when we examine potential regulatory failures.

The path for successfully implementing Basel II in any particular jurisdiction assumes a number of critical factors. It is not possible to conceive of every factor before it arises; our list is not meant to be exhaustive, but indicative of the hurdles which regulators are likely to face in executing administrative regulations based on Basel II principles. We also acknowledge that there have been three rounds in the consultative process with hundreds of participants[12] and that it would be safe to assume that practically every financial regulator in the world has issued both formal and informal comments regarding how each plans to respond to Basel II and whether it will implement the full breadth of the New Capital Accord. No one doubts that Basel II implementation is a tall order to fulfil. The following discussion of five critical risks entails a broad range of sub-risks. The five critical risks are

1   Unreasonably high and uncertain compliance costs
2   Bipolarity: negative and positive discrimination
3   Lack of certainty and stability of fundamental terms
4   Forum shopping and regulatory arbitrage
5   Regulatory amplification

each of which we discuss in turn.

Unreasonably high and uncertain compliance costs

It appears that regulators are not prone to determine realistic estimates of the cost of compliance before broadcasting the virtues of their proposed regulations to the general public. For example, Ferguson, the Vice-Chairman of the Federal Reserve, has stated that in the opinion of some critics 'an explicit Pillar I capital charge would upset the competitive balance with non-bank and foreign bank competitors', and that 'foreign regulators ... will be less aggressive in their rule enforcement than U.S. regulators'.[13] However, Ferguson points out that under Pillar III disclosure, any significant differences across banks will be noticeable, 'in the expectation that counterparties will penalize inconsistent risk measures'.[14] This rationalist economics argument is based more on theoretical presumption than hard evidence that in an increasingly competitive financial marketplace, risk measures will expose outliers. Because of the strong possibility of uneven regulatory application of the standards, these risk measures may form only very weak signals or be totally ignored by market participants. In any case, there is no definitive study which reflects the actual costs of complying with Basel II, which necessarily increases the complexity of the financial environment, and where the main increase in costs is itself driven by the regulatory requirements.

In the case of Basel II, we have yet to find a rigorous and credible independent assessment of total compliance costs per bank, and many back-of-the-envelope estimations appear to be widely circulated. For example, Charles Freeland, Deputy Secretary General of the Basel Committee for Banking Supervision, felt compelled to write a letter to the British Bankers Association correcting their published figure of $15,000 billion for compliance costs of Basel II. This appears to be calculated simply taking $500 million per bank (which appears extravagant) and multiplying it by 30,000 banks.[15]

Informal assessments have an extremely wide range – from a few man-years for a small-to-medium sized German bank to thousands of man-years for large internationally active banks. One figure attributed to the Barclays Group is that they estimate spending £100 million before fully implementing their Basel II programme.[16] As a thumb-nail estimation, let us say that Basel II implementation costs are approximately 1 per cent of the total turnover of the bank, until final full implementation, which will take approximately four years, after which this exceptional-cost item is completely absorbed within the profit margin of the bank. This figure on a global basis would reach into the many billions of dollars, but would be considered just part of the modernization cost of banks. But this is simply a hopeful scenario with very little calibration. In another study estimating the costs of Basel II compliance, the information technology costs associated with upgrade, disaster recovery, and cost of building a back-up facility could be as much as $30 million for a mid-sized bank.[17]

Giles and Milne (April 2004) conducted an insightful analysis of Basel II costs in terms of comparing the additional costs of implementing a basic or standardized approach versus the more advanced approaches. They questioned the assumption that banks should undertake investment in the more sophisticated approaches to credit risk and operational risk. On their calculation, using a weighted average cost of capital model, they estimated the risk-adjusted change in funding balancesheets and comparing this with the cost of implementing the advanced internal-risk-based approach for credit risk. They found the short-term costs to be about 5 basis points, which greatly exceeded their estimate for the short-term aggregate benefit of 0.4 basis points.[18] They note that Oliver Wyman currently estimates that the cost for large banks is of the order of £100–200 million or 5 basis points of their asset base.[19] Chorafas (2004), who has interviewed a number of banks which have established credit-risk and market-risk programmes, says that estimates of total implementation costs of Basel II are within the $50–100 million range.[20] Brett (2003) conducted a survey of large European banks and found that the average estimate for compliance with Basel II over five years is   115 million.[21] Note, however, that these estimates are for very large banks. For smallish banks, Freeland (2004) estimates $100,000 to implement a basic approach.[22] Depending on the size of bank, Karen Van de Castle estimates variance in total cost from $1million to $100 million.[23] HSBC officials have confirmed that its cumulative cost of compliance to Basel II has surged to $400 million,[24] while PricewaterhouseCoopers reported that European banks have already spent $6 billion to achieve compliance with the new banking regulations.[25]

Freeland (2004) has also estimated the consulting costs of major change programmes for large financial institutions. If we assume that the bank needs to establish an analytical centre and a data-warehousing facility to provide access to relevant data, to ensure that automaticity (that is 'enter once, use many times') is incorporated, and that processes and controls are sufficiently detailed and mapped down to the transactional level, then the implementation project costs per bank could involve many hundreds of man-days of experts and costs attendant to software systems integration. Banks are expected to spend the largest proportion of their budgets on data warehousing, with a specific focus on data consistency and processing systems for ATMs and check clearing.[26] Vendor estimates for Basel II compliance solutions range from $300,000 to $1 million for banks with adequate IT infrastructures in place. For banks without proper infrastructure in place, the process of achieving Basel II compliance could cost from $2 million to $3 million.[27] In many cases, the skills of existing staff will need to be upgraded, also upgrading of regulatory reporting and IT systems at the supervisory authority or central bank may be needed. These efforts may involve creative methods for attracting, upgrading and retaining qualified staff, and will also involve external auditors, internal auditors and consultants.[28]

Due to this potentially large range and magnitude of expenses and investments, we agree with Giles and Milne (2004) that the benefits of sophisticated compliance need to be considered in the light of strategic business risks and, undoubtedly, reputational risk. For highly regarded institutions, compliance with Basel II advanced risk approaches is seen as an essential part of their institution's market credibility.

Suppose the costs of compliance range from extremely high to low, what does it matter in relation to regulatory failure? Would it not be reasonable to expect that a market level would be established for compliance costs? The point is that the large differential in compliance costs between the fundamental approach and the advanced approach explicitly reinforces the division between 'inferior' and 'superior' risk approaches. In the USA, the regulatory authorities have either inadvertently or consciously neglected this argument in favour of the policy of a 'balance costs versus benefits' view, and have agreed to implement only the most advanced Basel II options and to limit the number of required participants to top-level 'opt-in' banks.[29] Banks which are not allowed to opt in may be strapped with a regulatory label that stands for 'second-rate' or 'non-existent risk management systems'. Should the unfairly labelled banks sue the regulator for attempting to implement regulations which set unreasonably high barriers to credible risk management? The potential deterioration of reputation caused by banks labelled as 'basically impaired' by the ranking system of Basel II means that these banks could be driven out of business.[30] Their opportunity to be compensated for this 'unjust taking' of reputation would require novel legal arguments, and therefore their chances of winning in court could be very small indeed. However, less-capable banks attempting to climb the steep slope of appropriate and non-trivial risk management development would find their efforts in vain since their reputations may suffer from inadequate execution of their programmes. Thus, there would be even less incentive for banks at the margin to try to improve their systems. From a practical and conservative management perspective, attempting even incremental improvements would be unsupportable and unjustifiable. This means that at one end of the economic spectrum of banks we have the potential of total regulatory failure.

In order to overcome or manage this risk, our recommendation is that regulators must work rather hard to promote the virtues of the basic and fundamental approaches in order to dampen the low opinion that these approaches carry. They must also somehow convince investors, governments and financial institutions which will have advanced risk-management systems that their less-advanced brethren are worthy of trading relationships. Needless to say, by virtue of the very structure of the Basel II framework this is a very difficult pitch to sell because it appears to be in direct opposition to the obvious hierarchical nature of the framework itself. The nightmare scenario is that institutions undertaking the basic or standardized approaches are perceived to be *less crediworthy* because of their lack of sophisticated risk management. The basic approach while bluntly requiring capital to be calculated in a simple way, just as bluntly increases the reputational risk of the institutions that do so, and may inevitably drive some out of business. At some threshold point, this will implicate liquidity risk and could cause a catastrophic increase in the risk premia of a large number of smaller banks.

This wide variance in the compliance costs between the simpler and more advanced approaches implicates another potential failure of Basel II, namely the bipolarity of unfair negative and positive discrimination.

Bipolarity: the unfairness of negative and positive discrimination

Is bipolarity inherently fair? Applying a variant of Rawls second principle of justice, a law which is directed to a specific group should not be introduced wherein members of the group who are least capable of protecting themselves are harmed by the implementation of the law in question.[31] On this ground, the smallish banks do not appear to be unfairly discriminated by the implementation of Basel II, since Basel II takes account of their lack of resources and in a sense, exempts them from taking on the more expensive advanced approaches. Kashyap and Stein (2004) agree with this view, claiming that thousands of banks following current regulatory capital requirements will not experience competitive disadvantage, since amounts required to be held are generally below the actual amounts they hold in capital.[32]

However, this two-level playing field is further exacerbated by the transmission of reputational risk to parties which do not undertake the advanced approaches. To be labelled as a bank that takes on the foundational approach would be tantamount to a diminution of its credibility. The fact that Basel I was accepted throughout the world should not be used as an analogy for the take-up of Basel II. Basel I created a *higher level of credibility*, while Basel II is in effect establishing a *lower* and minimum base of compliance, which is a disincentive for implementation. The effect of Basel II's bipolarity is to reduce a great number of institutions' credibility to the lowest level, which entails perverse market effects. Although some theorists have argued *ad baculum* that even if central banks do not force the banks' hands, competitive pressures will.[33] Regulatory pressures may force banks out of business because of the unfair bipolarity of its conception. For example, smaller banks, may be forced by the market to hold capital above the well-capitalized banks' level, and therefore on a cost–benefit analysis, according to Olson (2003) would be very strongly against adopting Basel II from a business perspective.[34]

The argument runs that if a bank does not embrace advanced approaches because it cannot do so either due to regulatory prohibition or lax regulatory permission, then the bank's non-compliance with the advanced approaches is a sign of its incapability or weakness in terms of being able to manage its portfolio of risks. Banks operating in emerging economies are particularly susceptible to this argument; such banks seeking lending facilities will be charged higher interest rates, and paying high interest rates to borrow from overseas will force them to pass even higher rates to their domestic customers, rocketing the overall costs of borrowing.[35] Basel II's bipolarity reinforces the divergence and economic disparities found in emerging economies;[36] on the one hand encouraging a concentration of apparent creditworthy names,[37] while also lessening a genuine diversification of risks, and, ultimately, reducing the choice of market alternatives. One of the reasons smaller banks may recede is that Basel II allows for the recognition of physical collateral only under internal ratings-based approach (IRB) and not under the standardized approach. This means that smaller banks will be prevented from taking advantage of a natural credit hedge, yet again emphasizing Basel II's bipolarity.

From the point of view of depositors and other transactional counterparties, increased reputational risk could be detrimental to ongoing relationships with the bank in question. It is certainly the case that any perceived increase in reputational risk could adversely affect the flow of new business and, therefore, hamper the growth of small institutions. Whilst the intent of the Basel II's incentive-based system is to allow more choice along three tracks of scrutiny, the unintended consequence may be to deter small and medium-sized banks from any growth. If banks do not comply with Basel II, they could find themselves left out in the cold by the international lenders on whom they depend.[38] Basel II is also likely to promote mergers of smaller banks where the economic rationale for merging may become a matter of survival.[39]

This is not just a theoretical argument, for we note a letter dated 27 October 2003 by Kathleen Marinangel, President/CEO of McHenry Savings Bank, McHenry, Illinois addressed to Ms Jennifer J. Johnson, Secretary, Board of Governors of the Federal Reserve System, wherein the President/CEO stated:

> While talking to industry representatives I have found that there exists a misconception that community banks do not want to be forced to adopt the Basel II Accord as proposed. Please help get the message out that it is critical that we be allowed to 'opt-in' to this new proposal. The New Accord is trying to more closely link minimum capital requirements with an institution's risk profile. Community banks must retain the option to leverage their capital, regardless of the complexity of the calculations to prove their risk-worthiness. Small institutions will be at a competitive disadvantage to the extent that they cannot deploy capital as efficiently as larger, more sophisticated institutions.[40]

To be fair, under Basel II there is provision intended to protect small banks from 'prohibitive' costs; that is, specifically there is an option of partial use of IRB. However, the bipolarity persists since the disadvantage lies in the minimum capital requirements of the basic and standard approaches compared to those implementing the IRB.[41]

A rather perverse counter-argument is that banks which undertake a standard approach will be perceived to be more risky and should exhibit higher volatility of earnings. They would therefore appeal to a group of irrational depositors, investors and other counterparties who are looking for higher-risk returns. We believe that this outcome, while possible, has only *de minimus* likelihood.

Again, how could a regulator justifiably prohibit a bank from implementing a more sophisticated risk approach? It would be absurd in the extreme for the regulator to negate the free choice which is patently within the Basel II framework. Assuming this error in regulatory interpretation is corrected, there is still the problem of justifying the fairness of the scheme.

If, on the one hand, bipolarity unfairly discriminates against the competitive energies of smaller banks (that is, a form of negative discrimination), it also, on the other hand, offers protectionism to the much larger banks (a form of positive discrimination). The Basel II incentive to large banks is that in return for developing their own advanced models, the regulator will allow them a lesser regulatory risk charge based on the *bank's own model*. The important point is not so much the regulatory risk charge, since this is in any case usually lower than what a prudent bank would normally hold, but the very procedure under Pillar Two wherein the so-called supervisory review conducted appears to invite regulatory capture. Stress-testing and scenario-analysis are called for under Pillar Two, but how will the regulator adjudge the reliability of the bank's risk models? There is nothing within the body of Basel II to help regulators here. The question comes up again on the limits of the scientific competence of regulators. However, the fairness argument does not depend on superior knowledge, and should be solved by a fair administration of the two-tier system which, after all, merely mirrors the economic reality of the financial industry.

This 'mirror argument' might be more explicitly stated as follows: that because Basel II's incentive-based mechanism merely mirrors the already existent hierarchical concentration of capital in the few large institutions, it is *ex ante* fair. But the counter-argument is that Basel II does more than merely mirror, since, by virtue of regulatory actions of approval, it generates market signals that *reinforce* the hierarchical structure that contains this concentration. The incentive-based mechanism does nothing to eradicate the barriers to entry to advanced risk-management systems, and indeed heightens the barriers to entry by assuming that only the most sophisticated models by large banks are likely to be condoned.

Another counter-argument is that the explicit language of Basel II calls for a tripartite division, and thus a more graduated approach to risk-management sophistication. However, this is specious since the difference in sophistication between the first-to-second level of sophistication and the third level of sophistication is so great that the most advanced level represents a wholly different nature of risk management. Basel II also provides rewards for the highest approach by allowing banks to reduce risk capital via diversification benefits and netting. For smallish banks there are no such benefits, and therefore, again, the bipolar treatment and incentives will tend to exaggerate the unequal treatment of small versus big banks.

Bipolarity means unequal treatment, unequal privileges and unequal protection under the laws. Our recommendation to regulators is that they poll smaller and medium-sized banks before assuming they do not desire to partake of advanced risk-management approaches. And if they do wish to do so, they should be granted some benefits to defray their large start-up costs. This might be done in the form of transferable tax-credits or tradable permits calibrated against the total amount of economic capital which the total banking system should hold. Using the latter method, a specific amount of capital could be earmarked, valued and monitored by central banking authorities, which could then be tapped in case of exceptional risk events.[42] These measures would help right the balance more in the favour of smallish banks in this asymmetric playing field.

And at the other end of the market, the regulator needs to trim the protectionism offered to big banks. The 'too big to fail' syndrome is often used as justification for regulatory intervention, but it can also be viewed from a derivatives perspective as an option on moral hazard. Basel II big-bank favouritism and protectionism may come in the form of the regulator being dependent on the bank's judgment on the viability of its own advanced risk systems, its purported hundred million dollar investment in such systems, and the likely argument from the bank itself that it has spent too much money on risk compliance that it cannot be made to fail.

This is a variant of the 'too big to fail' argument used by regulators to justify violating rules against conflicts of interest, moral hazard and adverse selection. To be even more explicit, one can imagine a scenario, post-2007, wherein a sophisticated bank convinces its regulator that if the regulator were to invalidate its advanced risk-management approach, then it would send a catastrophic signal to the markets since then no other sophisticated bank would wish to follow suit. In other words, Basel II's bipolar structure carries the seeds of its own destruction. Notice here that whilst three consultation periods have been conducted for Basel II, most of the feedback to the consultative papers has come from sophisticated banks and think-tanks that serve this segment of the industry.

And, finally, imagine not just one bank at a time looking for the regulator to approve its sophisticated model, but *a group of big banks* together requesting that the regulator approve their 'common advanced approach model'. They may cloak their argument in terms of setting sophisticated standards, and they may even have new business process patents for their risk-management systems, but this oligarchic pressure of risk standard-setting will have the classic anti-competitive features of blocking entry to new participants. Since these risk models could strongly impact portfolio valuation, credit rating and investor confidence, it would appear unlikely that the regulator would be in a position under current Basel II provisions to deny this sophisticated group's request for what might be called 'even greater market dominance'. If the regulator were to concede this point to sophisticated players, then regulatory capture would be complete.

In order to avoid regulatory failure, we recommend regulators avoid even the slightest appearance of regulatory capture, since this would destroy the credibility of the regulator and put in jeopardy the full market acceptance of the Accord.

Lack of certainty, clarity and stability of fundamental terms

Basel II has undergone three consultative proposals and three quantitative impact studies attempting to calibrate the appropriate risk weightings and other regulatory parameters. To draw a simple analogy, one might think of this consultative exercise as an attempt to find the appropriate speed limit on highways. It is good that highway users are asked what they think are the appropriate speeds for particular roads and highways, since then there should be less controversy and more efficiency in the aftermath of setting new speed limits.

But this is not quite the case for Basel II's risk-based approach. A more properly drawn analogy would be that the Basel Committee is actually asking the financial community to help define the fundamental concept of motion including velocity and acceleration as it applies to various highways. More specifically, Basel II appears to assume that a general theory of risk can be used to determine the appropriate risk measures, which banks must use. And it is left for the banks to agree with their regulators exactly what the risk-measurement framework should be for the advanced approaches.

Under the advanced approaches of Basel II, banks must define the risk categories and methodology for measurement, and submit these for approval (Pillar Two requirements). Banks may even differ in their approach towards this calibration. So, how is the regulator going to decide between the various types of calibration based on differing sets of measurement methodology, that regulatory capital is actually what it says it is? This appears to be of unfathomable discretion on the part of the regulator.

For example, in the briefing report published 11 May 2004, the Basel Committee confirmed the calibration for credit risk to include only 'unexpected loss', and not 'expected loss'.[43] This was a clear win for those believing in economic capital models as the 'way forward' to risk integration, since unexpected loss is an essential building block to such model construction. This change has caused a recalibration of what constitutes capital and how it might be captured in Tier 1 (cash instruments) or Tier 2 (cash-like financial instruments) – basically half of the excess of capital derived from unexpected loss goes into the Tier 1 bucket, and the other half in the Tier 2 bucket. Since most highly rated financial institutions are more likely to deal almost exclusively in Tier 1 capital, this change in rule will give these banks pause to consider how they might take advantage of this rule change and to find ways to 'diversify' their portfolios so that they might hold higher-risk Tier 2 capital.

At a more fundamental level, one of the principal benefits of utilizing the advanced internal-ratings based approach for credit risk and the advanced measurement approach for operational risk, is the diversification effect. The Basel Committee is correct to be cautious about the purported diversification benefit that may be had from using models of commercial vendors and bankers. It is for this reason that the regulator's mantra is shifting from 'appropriate model' to 'data intensity'. Without appropriate data-sets to at least demonstrate diversification effects, the Basel Committee is right to be cautious, if not sceptical about purported results of models. This lack of data-sets has led not only to a delay in the implementation of Basel II, but also to the risk of dis-coordination. This risk is manifest because Basel II involves a 'one-year parallel phase' during which both new and old capital requirements will be in force; both regimes may cause confusion, and added layers of costs.[44]

Again, without specific clarity of what 'diversification benefits' may be attached to advanced approaches, and, more importantly, indicating what types of data-collection and modelling are appropriate to reliably reach these diversification benefits, then it is very difficult to imagine what a meaningful approach to meeting Basel II's highest standards might be. Or, to put it a bit more boldly, the breadth of regulatory discretion at this critical juncture is so great that it would allow for logically consistent approaches (models) that have low accuracy to be approved. One wonders how regulators will be able to perform the scientific assessment required in order to verify claims made by regulatees.

Our recommendation here is for regulators to pursue even more vigorously scientific assessments of critical definitions which may have commercial significance to regulatees; for example 'diversification benefits' and that specific models be published as 'benchmarks' which can be reconstructed and tested by any and all market participants. Without certainty and clarity on what constitutes 'advanced models', Basel II will be prone to accusations of vagueness likely to result in perceived instability in regulatory control, making it more susceptible to regulatory failure.

Another large part of Basel II which requires much better definition is the area of operational risk, insurance and business risk. We briefly mentioned the problem of the Basel II typology of operational risk in the discussion following Figure 2.1 above. Some authors have argued that 'the prospect of systemic consequences from operational losses in investment management companies is negligible', and that '...an alternative policy based on private insurance and process regulation to regulate operational risk is superior to capital regulation'.[45] This may be true, and it is certainly the case that the Basel Committee is attempting to find some way of bridging insurance to the operational risk charge. The current proposal of allowing the notional amount of insurance to be deducted to 75 per cent of the value of the standardized operational risk charge appears arbitrary. Why not the full amount and consider the insurance a form of Tier 2 or 3 capital? We wonder whether the Basel Committee perhaps simply did not consult in depth with their counterparts representing the insurance industry. To return to Figure 2.1

above, it appears extraordinary to have to emphasize the simple point that non-financial risks should be regulatory assessed but not risk-charged, since by definition non-financial risk whilst detectable is not necessarily controllable by the regulator or the regulatee.

We stated that Basel II explicitly excludes consideration of medium-term business economic risks, such as reputational risk and strategic business risks. This gap in the regulatory regime can perhaps be better understood in terms of very short-term volatility (for example price to next price, or observable action to next observable action in a functional process). We suggest that the non-financial risks as a whole defined in Figure 2.1 be used to completely replace the concept of operational risk as it is defined in Basel II. We also suggest that at the very least, non-financial risk be divided into 'time buckets' so that very short-term volatility is related to liquidity risk, immediate effects of a shock to an internal system factor be calculated in terms of basis points, and that medium-term effects caused by macro-business economic factors be calculated on a medium-term frequency, say quarterly or annually. Thus, the very short-term would correspond to the internal factors and liquidity risk, the external short-term shocks to the value of trading, and medium-term business-economic shocks related to the quarterly and annual profits or losses.

Forum-shopping and regulatory arbitrage

Whatever good Basel II provides by inspiring internationally active banks to improve their risk-management systems may be completely negated if internationally active banks are regulated in an uncoordinated fashion. We cite the BCCI case above as a case in point where a College of Regulators was agreed only eight years after the bank was in operation. In the 11 May 2004 communique by the Basel Committee, there was mention of developing 'home-host' rules;[46] and since these rules are to be announced in the near future, we reserve comment except to say that despite whatever rules are developed, we would expect certain jurisdictions to offer 'Basel II Havens', where 'Basel II Avoidance Schemes' could be 'legitimately developed'. To expect anything less in the financial markets where Pareto efficiency reigns would be irrational. By analogy consider the breadth and depth of legitimate offshore tax-avoidance schemes which are generally upheld because of the recognition of sovereignty. Each nation is free to make its borders safe for more efficient tax treatment. So the argument may run for Basel II capital-friendly jurisdictions.

Our recommendation here is that whilst internationally active banks may have legal entities for whatever purpose, that these legal entities submit to the jurisdiction of the leading (home) regulator, and that all other regulators in host jurisdictions be able to sue the internationally active bank in its home jurisdiction. In this way, all regulators will be able to coordinate their coverage of the international bank's operations without fear of regulatory arbitrage.

Regulatory amplification

Regulatory amplification may be defined as the acts committed in the normal course of business by the regulator which unintentionally heighten the risk of failure of the regulatees. These acts could be conceived of as the 'operational risks' of the regulator, which have a direct effect on the effectiveness and efficiency of the regulatory regime. These include strategic planning, project management, adequate resources in terms of competent personnel and information systems, and clear communications with regulatees. Examples of regulatory amplification would include sudden changes in the expected implementation schedule, unclear procedures for the resolution of disputes with the regulator, and simultaneous regulatory burdens without sufficient industry consultation. On the Basel Committee on Banking Supervision's own research it has been shown that financial regulatory liberalization appears to have generated similar patterns of bank failures in Norway, Sweden and the USA. 'Financial liberalization (deregulation) was a common feature of major banking crises often combined with supervisory systems that were inadequately prepared for the change.'[47] Whilst very large bank failures were deemed idiosyncratic – that is, due to fraud such as Barings and BCCI – others were due more to market risk factors, such as Herstatt.[48] However, country-wide bank failures have occurred in the past, where there has been a failure of banks to manage fairly basic concentration risk in real-estate lending.[49] This implies a wide failure in the coordination between central bankers and the local bank constituency.

Conclusion

Whilst arguments may rage about whether the level of choice and complexity of Basel II will actually prevent bank failures and reduce systemic risk to the banking system, there is no doubt that the effort of proving the validity and feasibility of the framework will require a step-change in banking operations and higher monitoring costs by regulators. The higher monitoring costs cannot be avoided and are likely to escalate as Basel II implementation gathers momentum in terms of data-gathering, supervisee–supervisor coordination, and adjustments to disclosure requirements. We have outlined some of the essential factors which regulators should take account of in this initial phase of implementation. The integration of global markets was no doubt assisted by the thousands of banks that accepting the standards of Basel I. The open question is whether, outside of the few hundred banks that have the internal resources and capability to comply with the highest standards of Basel II, the rest will be inspired to follow. Or whether, as we have argued, the bipolarity of Basel II will lead to an uneven distribution of monitoring costs and, ironically, a higher risk of destabilization between large established financial institutions and smaller financial institutions in emerging markets.

Notes

1. See Basel Committee on Banking Supervision (April 2003), 'Consultative Document: The New Basel Capital Accord' (hereafter referred to as CP3) http://www.bis.org/bcbs/cp3full.pdf
2. A. Day (2003), *Mastering Risk Modelling, a Practical Guide to Modelling Uncertainty with Excel* (London: *Financial Times* – Prentice Hall), p. 325.
3. See generally D.N. Chorafas (2004), *Economic Capital Allocation with Basel II, Cost, Benefit and Implementation Procedures* (Amsterdam: Elsevier Butterworth Heinemann); and Economic Capital (EC) Subgroup of the Society of Actuaries Risk Management Task Force (March 2004) 'Specialty Guide on Economic Capital' http://rmtf.soa.org/specialty-guide-ecv1.5.pdf
4. BCBS (June 2004), Basel II, paragraph 677, p. 148, available at http://www.bis.org/publ/bcbs107.pdf
5. Basel II, paragraph 644, p. 137.
6. UK FSA (February 2003), 'The Firm Risk Assessment Framework', available at http://www.fsa.gov.uk/pubs/policy/bnr_firm-framework.pdf
7. See C. Borio (2003), 'Towards a Macroprudential Framework for Financial Supervision and Regulation?' BIS Working Papers no. 128 (February), p. 2.
8. J. Tanega (2004), 'Bank Failures and the Scope of Regulatory Control'; Basel II: Avoiding Regulatory Failure, Conference Proceedings, Global Risk Management Conference, University of Westminster, London.
9. See 'Bi-Polarity: The unfairness of Negative and Positive Discrimination', p. 22.
10. Vilfredo Pareto (1906), *Manual of Political Economy*; 1971 translation of

1927 edition (New York: Augustus M. Kelley). Pareto (at p. 261) states:

> We will say that the members of a collectivity enjoy *maximium ophelimity* in a certain position when it is impossible to find a way of moving from that position very slightly in such a manner that the ophelimity enjoyed by each of the individuals of that collectivity increases or decreases. That is to say, any small displacement in departing from that position necessarily has the effect of increasing the ophelimity which certain individuals enjoy, and decreasing that which others enjoy, of being agreeable to some, and disagreeable to others.

11. The Economist.Com at http://www.economist.com/research/Economics/alphabetic.cfm?TERM=RENT
12. See www.bis.org for the feedback responses to the consultative documents.
13. W. Ferguson (27 Feb. 2003), 'Testimony of Vice Chairman Roger', The Federal Reserve Board, available at: http://www.federalreserve.gov/boarddocs/testimony/2003/200302272/default.htm#pagetop
14. *Ibid.*
15. C. Freeland (5 Jan. 2004), 'The Costs of Basel II Implementation', *The Banker*, p. 104. Available at: http://www.thebanker.com/news/fullstory.php/aid/987/The_costs_of_Basel_II_implementation.html
16. N. Chorafas (2004), *Economic Capital Allocation with Basel II, Cost, Benefit and Implementation Procedures* (Amsterdam: Elsevier Butterworth Heinemann.), p. 22.
17. R. Dean, 'Basel II Heralds Huge Banking Reforms, the New Basel II Bank Regulations Herald a Huge Shakeup of the Arab Financial Sector', Dubai, available at http://www.ameinfo.com/news/Detailed/46768.html
18. T. Giles and A. Milne (April 2004), 'Basel II and UK Banks. What are the Costs and Benefits of IRB Qualification?' pp. 7–8, Finance and Financial Products, EU Financial Practitioner Papers, http://www.continuitycentral.com/baselpaper.pdf
19. *Ibid.*, p. 8.
20. N. Chorafas (2004), *Economic Capital Allocation with Basel II, Cost, Benefit and Implementation Procedures* (Amsterdam: Elsevier Butterworth Heinemann), p. 23.
21. R. Brett and T. Torris (20 August 2003), 'Basel II: Benchmarking the Costs of Compliance', available at http://www.forrester.com/ER/Research/Brief/Excerpt/0,1317,32297,00.html
22. C. Freeland (2004), p. 104.
23. Karen Van de Castle, p. 2, available at http://www.garp.com/garpriskreview/download/CreditRiskSP.pdf
24. E. J. Silverman (8 Oct. 2004), 'Asia – Basel II Expenditures for IT Infrastructure Constitute Majority of Compliance Costs', available at http://www.garp.com/risknews/newsfeed.asp?Category=21&MyFile=2004-10-08-9524.html
25. *Ibid.*

26. *Ibid.*
27. *Ibid.*
28. Basel Committee on Banking Supervision (July 2004), 'Implementation of Basel II: Practical considerations – July 2004', p. 3, available at http://www.bis.org/publ/bcbs109.pdf#xml=http://search.atomz.com/search/pdfhelper.tk?sp-o=1,100000,0
29. M. W. Olson (10 April 2003), 'Basel II: Its Implications for Second-Tier and Community-Size Banks', The Federal Reserve Board, available at http://www.federalreserve.gov/boarddocs/speeches/2003/20030410/default.htm
30. *Ibid.*
31. J. Rawls (1999), *A Theory of Justice*, rev. edn (Cambridge, Mass.: Belknap Press). See especially pp. 52–65 on the 'second principle of fairness'.
32. A. K. Kashyap and J. C, Stein (2004), 'Cyclical Implications of the Basel II Capital Standards' *Economic perspectives*, vol. 28(1), pp. 18–31.Available at: http://post.economics.harvard.edu/faculty/stein/papers/basel-chicago-fed-04.pdf
33. R. Dean, 'Basel II Heralds Huge Banking Reforms, the New Basel II Bank Regulations Herald a Huge Shakeup of the Arab Financial Sector', Dubai, available at http://www.ameinfo.com/news/Detailed/46768.html
34. M. W. Olson (10 April 2003), 'Basel II: Its Implications for Second-Tier and Community-Size Banks', The Federal Reserve Board, available at http://www.federalreserve.gov/boarddocs/speeches/2003/20030410/default.htm
35. R. Dean 'Basel II heralds huge banking reforms, the new Basel II bank regulations herald a huge shakeup of the Arab financial sector', Dubai, Available at: http://www.ameinfo.com/news/Detailed/46768.html
36. *Ibid.*
37. *Ibid.*
38. *Ibid.*
39. *Ibid.*
40. K. Marinangel (27 Oct. 2003), Letter to Ms. Jennifer J. Johnson, Secretary Board of Governors of the Federal Reserve System. p. 1. Available at http://www.federalreserve.gov/SECRS/2003/November/20031110/R-1154/R-1154_88_1.pdf
41. A. K. Kashyap and J. C, Stein (2004), 'Cyclical Implications of the Basel II Capital Standards' *Economic perspectives*, vol. 28(1), pp. 18–31.
42. The financial structure of such permits are not difficult to imagine since they would be government-backed triple-A bonds with embedded options related to macro-economic events. This type of macro-economic derivative products which are freely tradable risk-capital could be used to counter-balance procyclicality. See R. J. Shiller (2003), *The New Financial Order, Risk, in the 21st Century* (Princeton and Oxford: Princeton University Press).
43. Bank of International Settlements (11 May 2004), 'Consensus Achieved on Basel II Proposals', available at http://www.bis.org/press/p040511.htm

44. D. Vangel (9 Oct. 2004), 'Risk, Governance Compliance Should Be a Communal Effort', *American Banker*, vol. 169, issue 175, p. 1, available at http://www.ey.com/global/download.nsf/US/American_Banker_Sept_10/ $file/AmericanBanker_091004b.pdf
45. C. W. Calomiris and R. J. Herring (Sep. 2002), 'The Regulation of Operational Risk in Investment Management Companies', in *Perspectives*, vol. 8(2), p. 2, available at http://www.ici.org/pdf/per08–02.pdf
46. *Ibid.*
47. Basel Committee on Banking Supervision (April 2004) 'Bank Failures in Mature Economies', p. 66, available at http://www.bis.org/publ/ bcbs_wp13.pdf
48. *Ibid.*
49. *Ibid.*

References

Bank of International Settlements (2004) 'Consensus Achieved on Basel II Proposal' (May), available at http://www.bis.org/press/p040511.htm
Basel Committee on Banking Supervision (January 2001) 'The Internal Ratings-Based Approach', available at http://www.bis.org/publ/ bcbsca05.pdf
Basel Committee on Banking Supervision (April 2003) 'Consultative Document; The New Basel Capital Accord', available at http://www.bis.org/ bcbs/cp3full.pdf
Basel Committee on Banking Supervision (April 2004) 'Bank Failures in Mature Economies', p. 66, available at http://www.bis.org/publ/ bcbs_wp13.pdf
Basel Committee on Banking Supervision (June 2004) 'International Convergence of Capital Measurements and Capital Standards', available at http://www.bis.org/publ/bcbs107.pdf
Basel Committee on Banking Supervision (July 2004) 'Implementation of Basel II: Practical Considerations', available at http://www.bis.org/publ/ bcbs109.pdf#xml=http://search.atomz.com/search/pdfhelper.tk? spo=1,100000,0
Borio, C. (2003) 'Towards a Macroprudential Framework for Financial Supervision and Regulation?' *Bank for International Settlements*, Working Papers, no. 128. available at http://www.bis.org/publ/work128.pdf
Brett, R. and Torris, T. (2003) 'Basel II: Benchmarking The Costs of Compliance.' Forrester, available at http://www.forrester.com/ER/ Research/Brief/Excerpt/0,1317,32297,00.html
Calomiris, C. W. and Herring, R. J. (2002) 'The Regulation of Operational Risk in Investment Management Companies, *In Perspective*, vol. 8(2), p. 2.
Chorafas, N. (2004) *Economic Capital Allocation with Basel II, Cost, Benefit and Implementation Procedures* (Amsterdam: Elsevier Butterworth Heinemann).
Croughy, M., Galai, D. and Mark, R. (2001) *Risk Management* (New York: McGraw-Hill).

Day, A. L. (2003) *Mastering Risk Modelling, a Practical Guide to Modelling Uncertainty with Excel* (London: Financial Times – Prentice Hall).

Dean, R. (n.d.) 'Basel II Heralds Huge Banking Reforms, the New Basel II Bank Regulations Herald a Huge Shake-up of the Arab Financial Sector', Dubai, available at http://www.ameinfo.com/news/Detailed/46768.html

Economic Capital (EC) Subgroup of the Society of Actuaries Risk management Task Force (March 2004) 'Specialty Guide on Economic Capital', available at http://rmtf.soa.org/specialty-guide-ecv1.5.pdf

European Association of Craft Small and Medium Sized Enterprises (UEAPME) (18 November 2002) 'Basel II Position Paper', available at http://www. ueapme.com/docs/pos_papers/2003/0301_Basel%20II_workingdoc_ Positionpaper.doc

Ferguson, W. (February 2003) 'Testimony of Vice Chairman Roger, The Federal Reserve Board', available at http://www.federalreserve.gov/boarddocs/ testimony/2003/200302272/default.htm#pagetop

Freeland, C. (January 2004) 'The Costs of Basel II Implementation', available at http://www.thebanker.com/news/fullstory.php/aid/987/The_costs_of_ Basel_II_implementation.html

Giles, T. and Milne, A. (March 2004) 'Basel II and UK Banks: What are the Costs of the Benefits of IRB Qualification?', Finance and Financial Products EU Practitioner Papers, available at http://www.continuitycentral. com/ baselpaper.pdf

Kashyap, A. K. and Stein, J. C. (2004) 'Cyclical Implications of the Basel II Capital Standards', *Economic Perspectives*, vol. 28(1), pp. 18–31.

Kettel, B. (1999) *What Drives Financial Markets* (London: Financial Times – Prentice Hall).

Lereah, D. (July 2003) 'Re: The Third Consultative Paper on the New Basel Capital Accord, Letter from National Association of Realtors to Basel Committee on Banking Supervision', available at http://www.realtor.org/ NCommSrc.nsf/pages/CommentsOnBaselII.

Marinangel, K. (Oct. 2003), 'Letter to Ms Jennifer J. Johnson, Secretary Board of Governors of the Federal Reserve System', p. 1, available at http://www. federalreserve.gov/SECRS/2003/November/20031110/R-1154/R-1154_ 88_1.pdf

Olsen, M. W. (April 2003), 'Basel II: Its Implications for Second-Tier and Community-Size Banks', The Federal Reserve Board, available at http:// www.federalreserve.gov/boarddocs/speeches/2003/20030410/default.htm

Paul, C. and Montagu, G. (2003) *Banking and Capital Markets Companion*, 3rd edn (London: Cavendish).

Reid, W. and Myddelton, D. R. (2000) *The Meaning of Company Accounts*, 6th edn (London: Gower).

Shiller, R. J. (2003) *The New Financial Order, Risk, in the 21st Century* (Princeton and Oxford: Princeton University Press).

Silverman, J. E. (October 2004) 'Asia – Basel II Expenditures for IT Infrastructure Constitute Majority of Compliance Costs', available at http://www.garp.com/risknews/newsfeed.asp?Category=21&MyFile=2004- 10-08-9524.html

Tanega, J. (2004) 'Bank Failures and the Scope of Regulatory Control', in Basel II: Avoiding Regulatory Failure, Conference Proceedings, Global Risk Management Conference, University of Westminster, London (June).

The Economist.com at http://www.economist.com/research/Economics/ alphabetic.cfm?TERM=RENT

Van de Castle, K. (n.d.) Director of Credit Risk Services S&P Solutions, Standard & Poor's Group, 'Credit Risk Management, Gaining Prominence in the Global Banking Industry', available at http://www.garp.com/garpriskreview/ download/CreditRiskSP.pdf

Vangel, D. (2004) 'Risk, Governance Compliance Should Be a Communal Effort', *American Banker*, vol. 169 (175).

Walsh, C. (2003) *Key Management Ratios*, 3rd edn (London: Pearson).

3
Developing an Understanding of Credit-Risk Processes in Selected UK Sectors

*Ann Puri and Harry Thapar**

Introduction

Over the years, the structural form model used by Moody's KMV Company has proved popular in the financial services sector. The commercially available model has provided a meaningful approach to reconcile credit ratings, with a market-based credit measure containing information about probability of default. Structural form models have several advantages; strong theoretical underpinnings based on a contingent claims approach. These approaches utilize stockmarket data that inherently contain forward-looking estimates about company earnings and investor risk expectations. However, the structural form method requires proprietary information and access to large historic data-sets about the company, industry and the market. These may not be readily available to a corporate financial risk manager. The manager may be focused on his company and his immediate industry, and may not have the detailed information required about static pools or the detailed knowledge about current or historic defaults in the wider market.

Our main aim in this empirical study was to utilize a company risk measurement method, based on a single-index market model. The market-based model employed information from equity prices and generated a company risk measure. The purpose of this was to

* We would like to thank Moody's KMV Company for giving us the permission to use their credit risk data, referenced from their Credit Monitor product, in this comparative study.

provide a cheap, but reliable method to monitor the performance of a company in response to policy changes. Thereafter, in a proactive way this could enable a company to intervene or develop strategies to mitigate credit-related risks. More importantly, as a diagnostic tool, information obtained from the simple model could be used to understand credit events that could potentially trigger processes leading to serious credit-rating migrations.

We have proposed a hypothetical credit-risk migration process model that depicts various stages of decline in credit performance. By interpreting both the Moody's KMV Expected Default Frequency (hereafter EDF) information, and that obtained from the company risk measure, it was possible to identify the various stages of the process.

The risks we calculated from the single-index model were initially mapped to the Moody's KMV EDF credit measure (referenced from their Credit Monitor product). Results were used to empirically interpret and monitor the credit-related changes that had taken place in publicly listed companies.

For full details of the Moody's KMV model and quantification of credit risk using the Merton (1974)-based approach, as implemented by Vasicek, see the review articles by Kealhofer (2003) and by Crosbie and Bohn (2003).

In the world of credit risk, Crosbie *et al.* (2003) and Kealhofer (2003) noted that the Merton (1974)-based model, as extended by Moody's KMV Company, has become a standard for default risk measurement.

A single-index market model is not new, but for our purposes it is effective in delineating risks into systematic and unsystematic components. In our case, the model was used to conduct event studies in credit-risk research at the individual company level. Knowledge about default histories was not required as it was assumed that a market was semi-strong form efficient; that is, it had already priced in historic information sets and all publicly available information. The model utilizes monthly logarithmic returns as key model inputs, and the method proved to be a good starting point to delineate macroeconomic and micro-risks. In order to assess the validity of this approach, and to gain a better understanding of the anatomy of the default processes, specific risks obtained for the single obligor credits were mapped and calibrated to a probability of default measure obtained from a commercial structural form model. In its many variants proposed by Kim *et al.* (1993), Longstaff and Schwartz (1995) and others, the structural form approach attempts to directly model the borrower's balance sheet. A firm's liabilities are seen as a barrier point for the value of the firm's assets. The results of the Crosbie *et al.* (2003) EDF measure are commercially available and were referenced from Moody's Credit Monitor product. The structural form model utilizes a market-based methodology as in Crosbie *et al.* (2003), consistent with the approach taken to generate specialized risk information contained in equity prices. Since market-based data have expectations components in them, in theory it is possible to identify any expected changes in credit-rating migration. The Crosbie *et al.* (2003) approach utilizes information about asset values (business value of the firm), asset volatility (business risk) and the default point (liabilities due), to determine a key default parameter called the distance to default. The distance to default of a firm was mapped to a database of empirical frequencies of similar distances to default companies so that a definitive measure of the probability of risk – the Crosbie *et al.* (2003) EDF measure – for a firm was obtained.

The asset value of the firm was obtained using an options-based contingent-claims methodology. The implied asset value of the firm was calculated from knowledge about the equity prices and information about the future cash-flows of the firm embedded in the equity price. Asset values were based on the underlying value of the firm that was independent of the firm's liabilities. Option theory was used to determine the market value of assets because the market value of debt was not known; the market value of assets was calculated by knowing only the market value of equity and the present value of liabilities. Asset volatility was also determined from an options-based model. It reflects the uncertainty with which the future cash-flows of the firm can be predicted by the market. In their papers, Crosbie *et al.* (2003) also noted that asset volatility was affected by company size and industry (2000). The measure was calculated as an annualized standard deviation of percentage changes in the market value of assets; thus:

EDF = (number of firms that have defaulted with asset values within two standard deviations of debt service)/(total population of firms within two standard deviations from debt service)

The formula for the distance to default (measured in standard deviations) used information about the difference between the market values of assets and the level of debt known as the default point. The default point took into account all of the short-term debt and 50 per cent of the long-term liabilities:

distance to default = (market value of assets − default point)/ (market value of assets × asset volatility)

When the market value of assets was less than the default point, the firm was assumed to have defaulted on its debt.

Methodology

Equity prices were used in our study. Given that equity markets exhibit semi-strong form efficiency, any credit-related information was assumed to be rapidly assimilated in the security prices. The single-index model formed the basis of an equity valuation model for the market. Information from the balance sheet and from other public sources was assumed to be rapidly incorporated in equity prices. If the extraneous market-related risks could be removed from the total risk, then in theory the remaining 'pure company risk' could be examined to see how well various credit-risk events were incorporated into security prices.

Monthly logarithmic returns were calculated for data covering the period from 1990–2003. The variances were determined for monthly return data over a continuous two-year time period, and results were expressed in variance terms. Conversion to annual standard deviation was achieved by taking the square root of the monthly variance and multiplying the result with the square root of 12.

Our long-term aim was to catalogue credit-related events obtained from individual firms and industries. This information could be compiled to develop a deeper understanding of the micro-mechanics and diffusion processes involved in credit-rating migrations across different industries.

Before this could be done, this study was undertaken to develop a set of tools to try and understand company credit-risk mechanics better. In this study, a schematic that represented our concept of the credit migration process, leading to default, is shown in Figure 3.1.

We assumed that from a range of factors that could potentially incapacitate a firm, a number of disparate and unrelated value-destructive

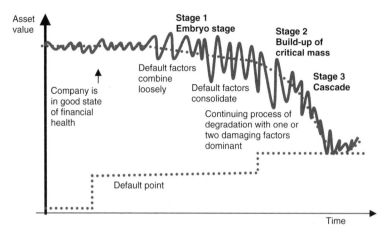

Figure 3.1   Schematic of the credit degradation process

factors needed to be present. These factors would initially act on the company to limit its growth opportunities (stage 1 – embryonic phase). Later, these factors would consolidate to erode any further growth possibilities (stage 2 – build to a critical mass). Unchecked, the factors would become firmly entrenched, and in time would conspire to destroy shareholder value (stage 3 – cascade phase), before finally leading to the failure of a firm.

To reverse the decline, some form of intervention would be necessary. The level of intervention and costs involved would depend on the timing and extent of the remedial action taken by the management of a company to selectively manage the destructive factors driving the process.

A single-index model

In a single-factor model, returns on an equity are assumed to be due to macroeconomic factors (m_i) and firm specific factors (e_i). The continuously compounded return over a holding period is R_i and the expected return is $E(r_i)$:

$$R_i = E(r_i) + m_i + e_i \tag{3.1}$$

Both m_i and e_i have zero expected values because each represents the impact of unanticipated events. Different firms have varying sensitivities to macroeconomic events, and the unanticipated component of the common macro factor is denoted by F. The sensitivity of the security to the macro event is given by beta, where:

$$m_i = \beta F, \text{ so} \tag{3.2}$$

$$r_i = E(r_i) + \beta F + e_i \tag{3.3}$$

In practice the market index was used as a proxy for the common macro factor. According to the single-index model the actual or realized rate of return on a security is separated into macro and micro components. The rate of return on each security is the sum of three components:

α_i, the stock's return when there was no anticipated change in the macro factor (that is, $r_m - r_f$ is zero);
$\beta(r_m - r_f)$ the component due to movements in the overall market; and
βi the security's responsiveness to market movements.

The unexpected component due to unexpected events relevant only to this security (e_i) holding period excess return was thus:

$$r_i - r_f = \alpha_i + \beta(r_m - r_f) + e_i \tag{3.4}$$

If excess returns are denoted by R:

$$R_i = \alpha_i + \beta R_m + e_i \tag{3.5}$$

This equation states that each security has two sources of risk – one from the market index and the other from firm-specific factors.

The variance of the excess return on the market R_m is $\sigma^2 m$; the variance attributed to uncertainty of the common macroeconomic factor is $\beta^2 \sigma^2 m$; the variance attributed to the uncertainty of the firm-specific micro factor is $\sigma^2 e$; and thus the total variance of a security is

$$\sigma^2 i = \beta^2 \sigma^2 m + \sigma^2 e \tag{3.6}$$

Since this is one of the popular models used in the pricing of equity securities, credit-related risks and other business risks that affect earnings growth expectations must be present and observable in equity prices. Our aim was to determine how the company risk could be calibrated to a commercially available structural form model, such as Moody's EDF. Although the single-index model lacks refinement, we believe that our credit-scoring technique may provide a cheap and reliable internal metric system to provide an early-warning system to corporate risk managers and financial planners.

In this report the telecoms and IT sector were studied in some detail because in 2001 the rapid expansion of the telecommunications industry, combined with increased liabilities in the sector, was followed by an equally rapid collapse of many firms in the sector. The failure of many firms was triggered by a number of factors. In a review of ratings performance of US companies carried out over the period from 1970 to 2001, Moody's Investor Services (2002) noted that a build-up of poor credit quality in the late 1990s bull-market, followed by an economic slowdown and terrorist attacks, created the conditions for a 'meltdown' of a number of firms in the sector. Their fate was sealed by the spectre of accounting fraud and mismanagement that increased uncertainty in financial markets.

We examined a large number of quoted firms using this model. To demonstrate the application of the model, a representative sample drawn from different sectors of the UK equity market are reported, and the results for companies in the telecommunications industry are presented in some detail. Similar observations from companies in another two sectors are presented to illustrate the role of the naïve single-index model in the measurement of credit risk.

In the telecommunications sector, we report on the following companies: Marconi, Telewest Communications plc and BT Group. In the utilities sector, Scottish and Southern Energy plc, a company that saw relatively few credit stress events, is examined. Finally, from the retail sector, the company Matalan showed only mild signs of credit stress in the time periods examined in this report.

Results and discussion

Marconi

In Figure 3.2, the relative share price performance of Marconi with the FTSE all-share index is illustrated for the period 1990–2004. The FTSE all-share index went into freefall in 2000 after the technology bubble burst.

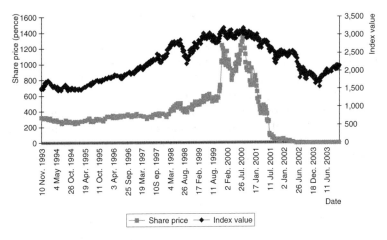

Figure 3.2   Relative share price performance of Marconi
Source: DataStream.

During the 1970s to 1990s, under Lord Weinstock's leadership, Marconi was largely a defence contractor and built itself a robust reputation as an ultra-conservative company. Lord Simpson took over as Chief Executive in 1996 and took a major gamble with the company. He set about changing the nature of the firm from a defence-related company into a more dynamic telecommunications business. In an effort to convert the business he went on a spending spree. The bull-run in the sector during 1999 encouraged firms to take on more debt, but when the telecoms bubble finally burst in 2000 the industry experienced a massive downturn, and Marconi saw its customer base (especially in the USA) dwindle. Lord Simpson hoped that the troubles in the industry and poor business conditions would prove transient, and in May 2001 he told shareholders that the market would recover around the end of the year. As the markets had already feared, his optimism proved to be wrong. Lord Simpson was forced to resign in September 2001 following failed attempts to revive the business and to reverse the decline. The company continued to remain in difficulty, and in March 2003 Marconi technically defaulted on its debt.

Marconi's S&P credit rating during the period is shown in Table 3.1. The credit performance of Marconi was also tracked over time using Moody's KMV Credit Monitor. Both the EDF and the market net

Table 3.1 Marconi's credit-rating migration

S&P rating	Comment	Date
BBB+	Adequate capacity to meet financial commitments	24 Feb. 2000
BBB−		06 Aug. 2001
BB		05 Sep. 2001
B+	More vulnerable near-term	21 Jan. 2002
B−		22 Mar. 2002
CC	Currently highly vulnerable	04 Apr. 2002
D	In default	19 Mar. 2003

Source: Standard & Poor's.

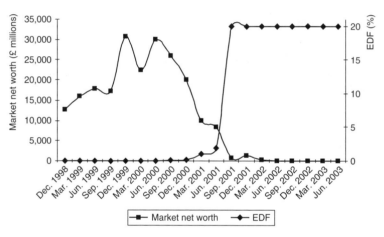

Figure 3.3   Marconi: Moody's KMV market net worth and EDF measures
Source: Based on data collected from Moody's KMV Credit Monitor.

worth measures (difference between the absolute measure of the asset value to the distance from the default point) are shown in Figure 3.3.

In September 2001, the EDF chart based on market expectations revealed that there was a 20 per cent probability that the firm would default within a year. Ratings lagged market views. The market net worth (difference between the market value of assets and the default point) was zero in June 2002, when the firm was effectively in default.

Using the single-index model, we determined the company risk by taking the difference between the total risk of the firm and market risk components, as shown in Figure 3.4. Figure 3.5 shows clearly that the company risk revealed similarities with information relayed in the EDF trend.

It is noted that company risks remained low up to September 1999, and then doubled from a low base in the period March 2000–December 2000. A trend shift was noted again in the first half of 2001, before a paradigm move in September 2001. Thereafter, as the company's credit position continued to get worse, company risk finally broke above the psychological 0.02 level (corresponding to 49 per cent volatility) in September 2001, to end on a record high of 0.069 (91 per cent volatility) by March 2003. The company was in technical default at this point. It is also important to note that the divergence between company risk and total risk signalled a trend change in September 2001. At this point the share price was clearly driven by company-related specific factors.

The naïve approach has the ability to pick up subtle credit-related events and shifts quite effectively. As far as Marconi was concerned, in the default process outlined in Figure 3.1, the company was at stage 3

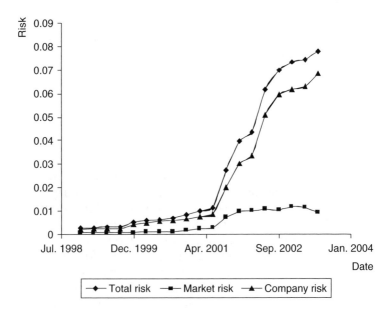

Figure 3.4   Marconi: risks over time

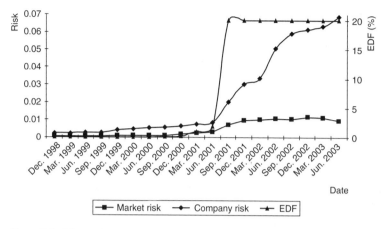

Figure 3.5   Marconi: comparing market risks with the EDF measure
Source: Based on data from Moody's KMV Credit Monitor.

(cascade process) by the second and third quarters of 2001. In mapping company risk onto the EDF profile, as shown in Figure 3.5, we note that in the fourth quarter 2001 and the first quarter 2002, from the EDF measure, there was a more than 10 per cent probability of the company defaulting within a year. According to our measure, the company risk at this time had already breached the 0.02 level, corresponding to an annual volatility of 49 per cent. This was a significant change in volatility. Note that in Sellers, Viasicek and Levinson (2000), Moody's KMV looked at asset volatilities for several industries of different asset sizes (see Appendix Table 3A). They noted that annualized volatilities for companies with total asset sizes of Stg 10,000 million and more were normally seen in a range from 0–25 per cent. In our case, from Figures 3.4 and 3.5, Marconi's annual volatility (as measured directly from equity prices) rose from a low base in July 1998 (13.9 per cent), to 35 per cent by April 2001. In 1996, annual volatility under Lord Weinstock's leadership was just 8 per cent. The move to an annual volatility of 49 per cent was a cause for concern and was unprecedented for a company of this position and size.

Telewest

Telewest Communications plc was also a troubled firm in communications and internet services. Results from both the EDF measure, and from our market model reveal that this company also had credit-related concerns (Figure 3.6). The company got itself into deep credit problems in the late 1990s, when, to build a strong business as a broadband communications and media group, management invested heavily in building cable networks and its internet business in the late 1990s. Building cable networks proved to be expensive, and the company had to take on higher debt levels at a time when the telecom and technology industry was facing difficult and testing trading conditions. When the telecoms bubble burst in 2000, the increase in asset volatility undermined asset values and brought the default point closer. By July 2002, asset values breached the default point and the company was in serious trouble. Restructuring efforts were underway from May 2002, and a deal was agreed in October 2002 when bondholders agreed to take control of 97 per cent of the company in return for canceling Stg 3.5bn of debt. The company defaulted on bond interest payments, and continued to rely on rounds of debt restructuring to keep the business afloat. The company risk in the first quarter of 2004 was at 0.081, corresponding to annual volatility of 99 per cent.

British Telecom

British Telecom plc is one of the UK's largest telecommunications companies. In August 1999, the company' share price was depressed

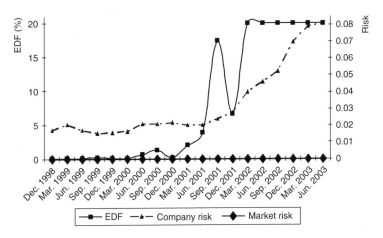

Figure 3.6   Telewest: evolution of market risks and the EDF measure
Source: Based on data collected from Moody's KMV Credit Monitor.

by Telewest's expected launch of a high-speed internet service. From February 2000, increased competition in the industry forced the company to shed 3,000 management jobs. The company continued to come under financial pressure as huge costs of securing the next generation of mobile phone licenses weighed on the company, and its debt burden reached Stg 30 billion by March 2001. It was difficult for the company to raise Stg 10 billion cash through flotation of its mobile phone company. By August 2001, the company had consolidated its position and launched a rights issue to raise Stg 5.9 billion in order to pay off its debt mountain. BT continued to restructure operations by de-merging its mobile arm MMO_2, and in April 2002 a strategic review revealed measures including fiscal discipline combined with increasing service levels to customers. Although BT faced troubles during 2000–01, the company was not considered to be at major risk of default, with good management and conservative leverage helping to keep a tight rein on the company's finances.

Both company risk and the EDF measure are shown in Figure 3.7, illustrating changes in the company's credit performance since 1998. The company was under a great deal of financial pressure in September 2002, seen in Figure 3.7 as a continuing rise in the trend of company risk during the period from June 2000 to the end of 2002, as well as increases in the EDF measure. With the risk at 0.005 in 2002 (annual

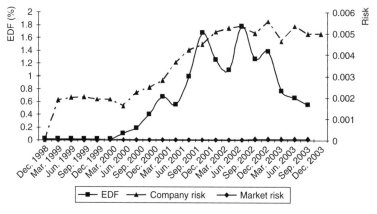

Figure 3.7   BT: evolution of market risks and the EDF measure
Source: Based on data collected from Moody's KMV Credit Monitor.

54

volatility 25 per cent), the levels were still lower than those witnessed for Marconi and Telewest Communications plc. Although the whole telecoms industry had been affected by the bursting of the telecoms bubble, company risk managed to stay well below the 0.02 barrier.

Retail sector: Matalan

Discount fashion retailer Matalan's risk profile was also charted, as in Figure 3.8. In the late 1990s to late 2001, the company saw its share prices rise and was regarded as Britain's fastest growing out-of-town retailer. Then in late 2001 and through 2002, a slowdown in the economy damaged sales and put a squeeze on profit margins, amid reports of boardroom clashes and disagreements.

In the first and second quarters of 2002, the EDF measure (Figure 3.9) rose from a low level, but signalled no major risks of default for the firm. According to the EDF, the probability of default was above 1 per cent, despite downturns in business trading conditions. Our own company risk profile remained in a broad sideways range (0.02–0.025) and did not signal any dramatic change in the credit risk trend for this company.

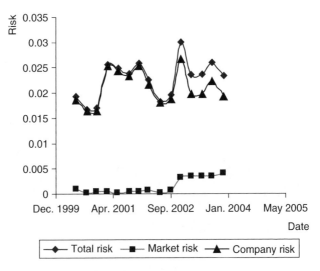

Figure 3.8   Matalan: market risks

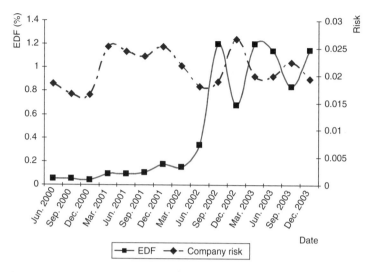

Figure 3.9 Matalan: evolution of market risks and the EDF measure
Source: Based on data collected from Moody's KMV Credit Monitor.

Utility sector: Scottish and Southern Energy plc

This sector was considered to be relatively safe from the high debt and credit-related problems that affected many companies in the telecoms sector. The relative share price performance against the FTSE all-share index (Figure 3.10) revealed that there were no major credit risks for this company. As a utility the company's stable financial position in the period 2002–03 was reflected by outperformance of the share price against the FTSE all-share index. This position was also captured by our company risk measure; both the EDF measure and our own company risk (Figure 3.11) were noted to have trended lower in the period from 2000–03.

Conclusions

Our study has demonstrated that the naïve market risk model results, when empirically mapped onto EDF trends, reveal a high level of consistency. The measure picks up the transitions in credit performance of companies very well.

The EDF measure was more sensitive to deterioration in company performance, and in a number of cases it hit its limit of 20 per cent in a

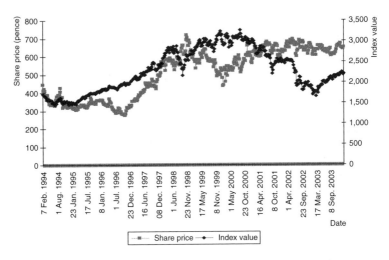

Figure 3.10 Relative share price performance of Scottish and Southern
Source: DataStream.

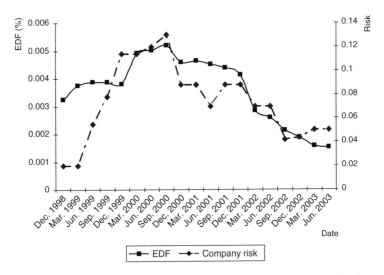

Figure 3.11 Scottish and Southern: evolution of market risk against the EDF measure
Source: Based on data collected from Moody's KMV Credit Monitor.

short space of time. Our simple model also picked up the subtle changes in company performance, but it was able to differentiate the transitions between the different stages in the credit migration process more fully.

For the companies reported, the 0.02 level of company risk acted as a significant threshold point. A firm that reached a company risk of 0.07 or more was considered to be close to default (corresponding to a 20 per cent probability of default within a year, according to the EDF measure).

The single-index model picked up the trends in the EDF measure well, although it is worth noting that there were some key differences in the volatility measures used in both models. It is important to note that asset volatility used in the computation of the EDF measure was related, but different to equity volatility (Sellers 2000). A firm's leverage has the effect of magnifying its underlying asset volatility. Sellers *et al.* (2000) contended that due to differences in leverage, equity volatility was far less differentiated by industry and asset size than is asset volatility.

In our work we have assumed that leverage affects were taken into account in the broad beta estimate used in the model. To improve the discriminatory power of the single-index model on an industry and company-size basis, it will be necessary in future work to fragment and analyse the company risk measure further. The impact of leverage on equity volatility also needs further investigation.

Appendix

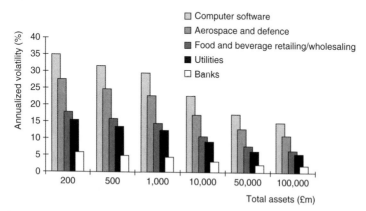

Figure 3A   Asset volatility for several industries and asset sizes
Source: Sellers, Vasicek and Levinson (2000).

References

Crosbie, P. and Bohn, J.R. (2003) 'Modelling Default Risk, Moody's KMV', available on website:http//www.moodyskmv.com/research/defaultrisk. html, accessed December 2003.

Kealhofer, S. (2003) 'Quantifying Credit Risk 1: Default Prediction', The Association for Investment Management Research (*AIMR*) (January/ February), pp. 30–44.

Kim, I.J., Ramaswamy, K. and Sunderesan, S. (1993) 'Does Default Risk in Coupons Affect the Valuation of Bonds?', *Financial Management*, vol. 22, pp. 117–31.

Longstaff, F. and Schwartz, E. (1995) 'Valuing Risky Debt: A New Approach', *Journal of Finance*, pp. 789–820.

Merton, R.C. (1974) 'On the Pricing of Corporate Debt: The Risk Structure of Interest Rates', *Journal of Finance*, vol. 29, pp. 449–70.

Moody's Investor Service (2002) 'Special Comment: Default and Recovery Rates of Corporate Bond Issuers', www.Moodys.com/cust/default.asp

Moscrop, J. (2004) 'Assessing the Probability of Default Using Moody's KMV Model', MSc dissertation, Westminster Business School, London.

Sellers, M., Vasicek, O.A. and Levinson, A. (2000) 'The Moody's KMV EDF Credit Measure and Probabilities of Default', working paper, KMV Corporation.

4

Risk Analysis and Sustainability of Alternative Crop Production Systems

Maqsood Hussain and Abdul Saboor

Introduction

Agriculture is the mainstay of Pakistan's economy. Being the lynch-pin of the country's economy, it continues to be the single largest sector and a central driving force for growth and development of the national economy. It accounts for 24 per cent of the GDP and employs 48.4 per cent of the total workforce. Agriculture contributes to growth as a supplier of raw materials to industry as well as a market for industrial products, and also contributes substantially to Pakistan's exports earnings (GOP, 2003). Almost 67.5 per cent of the country's population are living in rural areas and are directly or indirectly linked with agriculture for their livelihood. Any improvement in agriculture will not only help the country's economic growth to rise at a faster rate, but will also benefit a large segment of the country's population.

There are two principal crop seasons in Pakistan, namely the 'Kharif' sowing season which commences in April–June, harvesting during October–December; and the 'Rabi', which begins in October–December and ends in April–May. Rice, sugarcane, cotton, maize, bajra and jowar are 'Kharif' crops, while wheat, gram, tobacco, rapeseed, barley and mustard are 'Rabi' crops. Major crops, such as, wheat, rice, cotton and sugarcane account for 90 per cent of value added in major crops. The value added in major crops accounts for 41 per cent of value added in overall agriculture. Thus, the four major crops (wheat, rice, cotton and sugarcane), on average, contribute 37 per cent to value added in overall agriculture, while the minor crops account for 16 per cent.

Wheat is the main staple food and the largest grain crop in the country. It contributed 13.8 per cent to the value added in agriculture and 3.4 per cent of gross domestic product (GDP). During 2003, wheat was cultivated on an area of 8,176 thousand hectares, showing a 1.8 per cent increase over the previous year. The size of the wheat crop for 2003 was provisionally estimated at 19,767 thousand tonnes, 3.0 per cent higher than the previous year. The yield per hectare was also expected to increase by 1.2 per cent. Wheat production during 2003 was less than the target (20 million tonnes) by 1.2 per cent because of unfavourable weather during March. The shortage of wheat was the result of below-targeted production (Govt. of Pakistan, 2003–04).

In agriculture, the producer confronts two types of eventualities. One of these is risk, while the other is uncertainty. Risk means a situation in which the probability of obtaining some output of an event is known. In everyday usage, a risky situation is one in which one of the outcomes involves some loss to the decision-maker (due, for example, to either weather or tastes). Uncertainty reflects a situation where the probability of obtaining a given outcome is not known (Todaro, 1997).

Production risk is random variability inherent in a farm's production process. Weather, diseases and pest infestation lead to production risk in crop and livestock production, while fire, wind, and theft are other sources of production risk. Yield fluctuation is greatly influenced by weather and other uncontrollable factors, and risk and uncertainty influence the efficiency of resource-use in agriculture and decision-making processes. Anderson and Griffiths (1982) extended their multistage estimation approach for quantifying the impact of selected factors of production and empirical relationships in an analysis of the efficient allocation of resources. Thus, risk-bearing is concentrated among individual farmers and farm families, rather than spread over numerous corporate shareholders. In the case of several commodities, the low elasticities of prices and incomes that are subject to weather and other uncontrollable events cause wide swings in commodity prices. The effects of these factors combine to severely test farmers' risk-bearing capacities and thus obstruct their efficiency and welfare position (Barry, 1984). The mean net present values (NPVs) have been estimated for no-tillage and conventional tillage in the Brown Loam area of Mississippi. The mean simulated NPVs from zero tillage (ZT) were higher than for conventional tillage (CT), and, moreover, there was a higher level of variation in NPV from conventional tillage than from zero tillage (Hussain, 2000).

For the case of production risk, a risk-averse firm may produce more expected output and use more inputs than a risk-neutral firm (Loehman, 1992). The effect of risk-aversion on factor use is not positive for all inputs in general, but rather depends on the nature of the production process (Rulon, 1977). Risk analysis is rarely used in the estimation of production costs in the country, and it is due to this research deficiency that most of the policies in agriculture are not disseminating good results. If farmers' risk-bearing capacities could be evaluated beforehand, there would be a greater likelihood that precautionary measures could be taken to increase farmers' marginal profits. Aslam *et al.* (1993) compared zero-tillage wheat with conventional tillage wheat production in the rice–wheat zone of Punjab, Pakistan; wheat yield was 10 per cent higher in ZT production systems than for CT production.

Objectives

The main objectives of this study were the following:

1 To estimate the wheat production functions for zero tillage and conventional tillage.
2 To forecast the wheat production for zero tillage and conventional tillage systems.
3 To estimate the risk involved in both wheat production systems.

Methods and procedures

Our research was conducted to estimate wheat production, forecasting and risk analysis under two production systems. Zero tillage (ZT) is a sustainable crop production system that conserves the soil as well as resources, whereas conventional tillage (CT) leads to deterioration of the soil and is a non-sustainable crop production system. The district of Sheikhupura was selected as the focus of our study because wheat is the major crop sown in this area. The study is based on both primary and secondary data. A random sample of 100 farmers was selected from each of the two Tehsils (Sheikhupura and Ferozwala) of the district Sheikhupura; that is, 100 farmers for each production system. Hence 200 farmers were selected as respondents for this study. This random sample was selected after consultation with the staff of the agriculture department working in district Sheikhupura. Pre-testing of the questionnaire was done to assess its accuracy, during which many flaws and complications were found that were removed in the final questionnaire.

Production functions

Two production functions were estimated using ordinary least-square regression techniques. For the conventional tillage system:

$$CT = f\,(TNI, SR, DAP, Nit) \tag{4.1}$$

where *CT* is the conventional tillage yield of wheat (40 kg per acre), which is a function of: *TNI* the total number of irrigations; *SR* the seed rate (kg per acre); *DAP* the amount of fertilizer (number of bags per acre); and *Nit* a measure of soil fertility, nitrogen available in the soil (percentage).

The production function for the zero-tillage system is

$$ZT = f\,(TAIW, SR, DAP, Nit) \tag{4.2}$$

where *ZT* is the zero tillage yield of wheat (40 kg per acre), which is a function of: *TAIW* the total amount of irrigation water (acre inches); *SR* the seed rate (kg per acre); *DAP* the amount of fertilizer (number of bags per acre); and *Nit* a measure of soil fertility, nitrogen available in the soil (percentage).

Forecasting and risk analysis

Wheat production was forecasted for a period of 15 years, and BestFit, a companion product of @Risk, was used to find the probability distributions for the independent variables of estimated wheat yield production functions. By using 15 years of historical data for each of the independent variables of both the functions, BestFit provided the risk-normal distributions as the most appropriate distributions for these variables. These distributions contain two arguments – the mean and the standard deviation. @Risk performed the simulation analysis, using a Monte Carlo/Hypercube simulation for the risk analysis. Simulation means that a distribution of possible outcomes is generated by allowing the computer to recalculate the worksheet over and over again, each time using different randomly selected sets of values for the probability distributions. The computer solves the worksheets repeatedly using a large number of possible combinations of input variable values.

@Risk simulated the wheat yield over the planning horizon hundreds of times, each time calculating and saving the wheat yield that was computed with a particular sets of values of the wheat yield production function. In this way the forecasted wheat yield probability distribution for 15 years was constructed. Standard deviations measure the volatility of the yield around the mean or average yield. Most farmers would prefer less volatile yields to more volatile yields, other things being equal. The coefficient of variation (variability relative to the expected value or mean of the probability distribution) was also estimated to explain the variability.

Time often has a very important impact on estimates, they become less and less certain as projections extend into the future. To make the yield a random process, an uncertainty around the fixed trend of each production function was incorporated by adding an error term (root-mean-square error) to the fixed trend in the worksheet. In adding an error term to the fixed estimate, the mean of the error-term probability distribution should be zero. In all iterations of simulation, a new value for the error term was sampled for each cell and was used to add to the fixed trend estimate in that cell, allowing variation around the fixed estimate.

Comparison of CT and ZT wheat yield

The simulated forecasted wheat yield for both systems was compared to make a preferred choice; the mean wheat yield and its standard deviation provided enough information for this purpose. The simulated mean wheat yield was estimated over the 15 years and the coefficient of variation was estimated to explain the variability. This provides a method of evaluating the relative variability of any number of probability distributions that may have greatly different expected values. A smaller coefficient of variation means the distribution has less variability in relation to its expected value than other distributions (Kay, 1986).

Results and discussion

Production functions

The production functions estimated for both production systems using ordinary least-squares regression techniques are shown in Tables 4.1 and 4.2. The estimated wheat production function for conventional tillage (CT) is shown in Table 4.1, with the t-statistics of each estimated coefficient given in the last row of the table. The coefficient of determination (R^2) for this model was 0.697 for the wheat yield. The computed F-value of the model was 26.69. The results show that wheat yield was positively related to the quantity of seed (*SR*), the amount of fertilizer (*DAP*) and nitrogen (*Nit*), but negatively related to the irrigation variable (*TNI*). The negative sign indicates that, on average, farmers were providing at least one extra irrigation.

The estimated wheat production function for zero tillage (ZT) is shown in Table 4.2. The t-statistics of each estimated coefficient are again given in the last row of the table. The coefficient of determination (R^2) for this model was 0.677 for the wheat yield, and the

Table 4.1 Estimated wheat production function for conventional production system

	Constant	TNI (number)	SR (kg/acre)	DAP (bags)	Nit (%)
Coefficients	14.849	−2.062	0.348	9.229	7.595
t-values		−3.09	4.06	6.32	2.51

Table 4.2 Estimated wheat production function for zero-tillage production system

	Constant	TAIW (acre inches)	SR (kg/acre)	DAP (bags)	Nit (%)
Coefficients	3.230	0.009	0.704	4.420	10.290
t-values		0.04	3.34	2.03	2.12

computed *F*-value was 25.56. The results reveal that wheat yield was positively related to the quantity of seed (*SR*), the amount of fertilizer (*DAP*), nitrogen (*Nit*) and the irrigation variable (*TAIW*). There are many differences between the two production systems. Many tillage and intercultural practices are commonly carried out in the conventional tillage production system, while no such operations are performed in the zero-tillage system. Several agricultural implements are required for CT, but only a few implements are required in ZT. Hence the cost of initial investment is very much less in ZT as compared to CT. The zero-tillage planter aims to minimize soil disturbance and leave as much crop residue on the surface as possible. Tillage in the conventional tillage system kills weeds between crop rows, while in zero-tillage herbicide selection is more critical. As the soil is not disturbed at all in the zero-tillage system, so it conserves soil water, maintains the soil pores for aeration as well as colonies of soil biota. Because of intensive intercultural practices in the conventional tillage production system, soil water evaporates, soil pores and colonies of soil biota are destroyed.

Simulated mean wheat yield and standard deviation

Table 4.3 shows the results for simulated mean wheat yield for both the ZT and CT production systems over the 15 years' planning horizon. The mean wheat yield was greater in ZT (39.88) than CT (33.87), and the results show that as the planning horizon is increasing, the simulated wheat yield probability is also increasing, other things being equal. The standard deviation for CT was much larger than for the ZT production system. This higher level of variation in mean wheat yield for CT as compared to ZT can also be evidenced from the coefficient of variation (CV), also shown for both systems in Table 4.3. As the planning horizon increases, CV also increases in both systems, other things being equal. The increase in CV is greater in CT than in ZT, because the standard deviation is greater in CT than ZT. The smaller CV in the ZT system shows that ZT wheat production is less risky than CT. We also note that Triplett *et al.* (1996) found that average yields of zero-tillage cotton were 36 per cent higher than conventional tillage during the 1988–92 period.

The results for both systems have been presented in the form of distributions described by their mean and standard deviations. The stochastic simulation approach provides greater decision-making

Table 4.3 Simulation of mean wheat yield, standard deviation and coefficient of variation

Year	Conventional tillage			Zero tillage		
	Simulated mean wheat yield (40 kg)	Standard deviation	Coefficient of variation	Simulated mean wheat yield (40 kg)	Standard deviation	Coefficient of variation
2003	33.39	2.33	6.98	39.91	1.06	2.66
2004	33.96	2.63	7.74	39.92	1.25	3.13
2005	33.91	3.02	8.91	39.85	1.44	3.61
2006	33.98	3.26	9.59	39.93	1.68	4.21
2007	33.85	3.63	10.72	39.76	2.05	5.16
2008	33.97	4.07	11.98	39.86	2.43	6.10
2009	33.85	4.59	13.56	39.80	2.77	6.96
2010	33.87	4.93	14.57	39.84	3.20	8.03
2012	33.81	5.39	15.94	39.90	3.62	9.07
2013	33.98	5.67	16.69	39.94	3.96	9.91
2014	33.97	6.29	18.52	39.86	4.65	11.67
2015	33.66	6.66	19.79	39.95	4.98	12.47
2016	33.99	7.33	21.57	39.89	5.51	13.81
2017	33.81	7.95	23.51	39.98	5.90	14.76
2018	33.98	8.65	25.46	39.81	6.48	16.28

information, such as probability distributions of the wheat yield, which are not available from a deterministic model.

Summary and conclusions

The research was conducted in district Sheikhupura of Punjab, covering the two tehsils of Sheikhupura and Ferozwala to estimate wheat production, forecasting and risk analysis. Within these two tehsils there are three types of soils – clay, loam and clay-loam. Data were collected through questionnaires and interviews.

Zero-tillage wheat production has the potential to conserve soil water and reduce costs of production, and requires relatively very little initial investment cost. Simulated wheat yields were higher for ZT than for CT. To cope with uncertain values such as the availability of irrigation water in future, we used a Monte Carlo simulation for the risk analysis. Relative to the mean wheat yields, the standard deviation of CT was much larger than for ZT. This indicates that the CT system involves more risk than ZT wheat production. The higher level of risk in the CT system is also reflected in the coefficient of variation, which was found to be relatively larger in CT than ZT. Hence we conclude that zero-tillage (ZT) production systems should be preferred over conventional tillage (CT). The overall policy lesson that emerges from these research findings is that ZT, as a major resource conservation technology, should be promoted at a larger level in the country.

References

Anderson, J.R. and Griffith, W.E. (1982) 'Production Risk and Efficient Allocation of Resources', *Australian Journal of Agriculture Economics*, vol. 26(3) (December).

Aslam, M.A. Majid, Hashmi, N.I. and Hobbs, P.R. (1993) 'Improving Wheat Yield in Rice-Wheat Cropping System for the Punjab through Zero Tillage', *Pakistan Journal of Agricultural Reviews*, vol. 14(1), pp. 8–11.

Barry, P.J. (1984) *Risk Management in Agriculture* (Illinois: University of Illinois Press), pp. 24–5.

Govt. of Pakistan (2004) *Economic Survey 2003–04*, Finance Division, Economic Advisor's Wing, Ministry of Finance, Islamabad.

Griffith, D.R. *et al.* (1982) *A Guide to No-till Planting after Corn and Soybean*, Cooperative Extension Service Publication, ID-154 Purdue University, USA.

Hussain, M. (2000) *Economic Evaluation of No-tillage Cotton in the Brown Loam Area of Mississippi*, PhD dissertation, Department of Agricultural Economics, Mississippi State University, USA.

Kay, R.D. (1986) *Farm Management: Planning, Control, and Implementation*, 2nd edn (New York: McGraw-Hill).

Leohman, E. and Nelson, C. (1992) 'Optimal Risk Management, Risk Aversion, and Production Function Properties', *Journal of Agriculture and Resource Economics*, vol. 17(2), pp. 219–31.

Mohsin, M. (2004) *Estimation of Wheat Production, Forecasting and Risk Analysis with Special Reference to District Jhang*, MSc thesis, Department of Agricultural Economics, University of Agriculture, Faisalabad, Pakistan.

Palisade (2004) *Guide to Using BestFit*, Palisade Corporation, New York, USA.

Palisade (2004) *Guide to Using @Risk*, Palisade Corporation, New York, USA.

Rulon, D.P. and Richard, E.J. (1977) 'On the Competitive Firm Under Production Uncertainty', *Australian Journal of Agricultural Economy*, vol. 21(2) (August), pp. 111–18.

Todaro, M.P. (1997) *Economic Development*, 7th edn (New York: New York University Press), pp. 762, 768.

Triplett, G.B., Dabney, S.M. and Siefker, J.H. (1996) 'Tillage Systems for Cotton on Silty Upland Soils', *Agronomy Journal*, vol. 88, pp. 507–12.

5

Country Risk and Governance: Strange Bedfellows?

*Michel Henry Bouchet and Bertrand Groslambert**

Introduction: governance and country risk assessment

Enron, Worldcom, Vivendi and Parmalat, among many other examples, cast light on a lack of transparency and accountability, namely, bad corporate governance. Likewise, Cameroon, Turkmenistan, Argentina, Nigeria or Burma all constitute examples of dreadful sovereign governance. The combination of public awareness and better information has placed the issue of governance and government efficiency at centre-stage in political risk assessment. Country risk cannot be captured any longer by scrutinizing liquidity and solvency indicators or by

* After an international banking career at BNP, the World Bank and the Washington-based Institute of International Finance. Mr Bouchet was founder and CEO of Owen Stanley Financial, a specialized advisory firm dealing with debt restructuring strategy for country governments that became a subsidiary of ING Barings. He is Scientific Director of the MScIF programme at CERAM where he teaches International Finance and Country risk assessment. Graduated from the University of Paris in Economics and from IEP-Paris. Holds MA/PhD degrees in International Relations from USC. After working with Total-Senegal, Dr Groslambert joined Paris-based FP Consult, an emerging market investment management company with a US$250 million portfolio. He was equity fund manager specializing in Latin America stock markets. Dr Groslambert teaches International Finance Strategy and International Risk Management at CERAM. Graduated from CERAM, he holds a Doctorate in Economics from Aix-Marseille University. His areas of expertise include emerging markets and international economics. Bouchet and Groslambert are the authors with E. Clark of *Country Risk Assessment* (Wiley, 2003).

overrefining sensitivity analysis in balance of payments projections. Although governance emerged as a research issue in the academic community in the mid-1960s, it moved onto the front burner of the policy-making debates only 30 years later. Corruption was brought into the picture when scholars started to question the quality of the economic decision-making process and the allocation of the growth benefits. Issues of capital flight and economic inefficiencies were raised to assess the scope of 'Dutch disease' in countries where too much and too fast wealth is managed unwisely.[1]

What is governance? What is corruption?

The issue of governance is relatively new in international finance, emerging only in the early 1990s when the role of official institutions was put under the scrutiny of OECD countries' parliaments and NGOs. The latter challenged the international financial institutions (IFIs) as throwing taxpayer money at corrupt regimes and as bailing out incompetent governments in emerging-market countries. They raised the issue of 'governance' as a necessary criterion for determining eligibility access to public aid money.

Governance refers to sound public administration and service quality. It includes such issues as transparency, government accountability for the use of public funds, the rule of law, and social inclusion, according to former US Treasury Secretary Larry Summers (in IMF/ World Bank Development Committee, 2000). According to the World Bank in 1989, 'by governance is meant the exercise of political power to manage a nation's affairs'.[2] The World Bank refined and expanded its definition of governance in mid-2000 to stress the role of institutions: 'Governance includes traditions and institutions...'.[3] Efficient public-sector institutions are thus at the heart of good governance.

Corruption (from the Latin *corruptio* = decay) is one of the key criteria to assess the quality of governance. The World Bank has a short and straightforward definition of corruption: it is *the abuse of public power for private benefit* (Tanzi, 1998). This definition is widely used by scholars in the academic community.[4] It refers to the exchange and delivery of services for payments, privileges and undue compensations. In a way, something public (license, contract, tax break, subsidies, market share, bidding rights and so on) is exchanged or sold for private gains (speculation, insider information, cash payment, monopoly position ...). At the root of corruption is an arbitrary decision that translates into unfair comparative advantage. In the course of this chapter we define corruption as *rent-exacting power by public agency officials with a view of exchanging discretionary public preferences for private gains*. It involves a patron–client relationship.

Where does corruption come from?

There is no consensus between economists and risk analysts regarding the root causes and consequences of corruption. A first school of thought considers corruption as an inescapable, though temporary, fate in emerging-market countries; it is simply a 'normal' consequence of fast change in backward societies. Scholars such as Leff (1964), Lui (1985), Beck and Maher (1986), Lien (1986), Huntington (1968), Gamer (1976), Harberger (1988) and Charap and Harm (1999) argue in different ways that corruption is a byproduct of modernizing societies along the route towards the Rostowian 'take-off' stage of economic development. Corruption stems from weak institutions, but it can also result from the expansion of governmental regulation aimed at strengthening economic development. Harberger considers that bureaucrats cannot avoid pressures that stem from ties of family, religion, school, club and ethnicity. These ties constitute pervasive networks between government leaders, their appointees, and the clientele over which their authority is exercised. As Huntington summarizes: 'A traditional society may find a certain amount of corruption a welcome lubricant easing the path to modernization'.[5] Corruption performs a useful role to 'grease the wheels' of rigid social and institutional structures. It can even play a role in income redistribution in poor countries with rigid institutional fabrics. Corruption itself may be a substitute for reform. It serves to reduce social demands and group pressures for policy changes. As such, corrupt bureaucracies are an efficient form of rent-extraction for the ruling élite. Corruption buys time and creates adhesion. A similar stance, albeit with diametrically opposed conclusions, is found with Marxist scholars who analyse the role of the state in Third World countries in relation to the 'international division of labour'. Frank (1980), for instance, argues that corruption of élites has clear economic purposes to offer favourable conditions to international capital.[6]

The debate regarding corruption is polarized, indeed. A second approach looks at corruption as a suboptimal allocation of resources with a negative impact on growth. It devotes attention to bad governance, including reckless government spending, nepotism and crony capitalism, all leading to hidden subsidies, capital flight and ruthless speculation, resulting in conditions that precipitate crises. Corruption has adverse effects not just on state efficiency, but also on savings, investment and growth. Nye (1967), Rose-Ackerman (1975, 1978) as well as Shleifer and Vishny (1993) tackle corruption from a cost–benefit analysis angle, concluding that corruption is probably economically wasteful, politically destabilizing, and destructive of governmental capacity. Wei (1997), like Mauro (1995) and Tanzi (1998), points out that corruption boils down to an arbitrary tax that distorts markets and incentives, and it is likely to lower private investment and reduce economic efficiency and growth. Leite and Weidmann (1999) observe that countries which heavily rely on natural-resource exploration are more likely to feed corruption, as high rent activity tends to foster rent-seeking behaviour.

A third approach to corruption focuses on the consequences of bad governance on economic growth and financial crisis. In the mid-1990s, Krugman (1994) popularized the controversial view (also presented by Alwyn Young in 1995) that 'crony capitalism' undermines economic efficiency and creates fertile ground for financial crises. In the aftermath of the Asian debacle, Krugman (1998a, 1998b, 1999) stressed the role of moral hazard and bad governance related to implicit government guarantees on unregulated banks. Likewise, Roubini (1998) and Radelet and Sachs (1998) focused on the role of speculative short-term capital flows as crisis triggers, emphasizing the role of financial systems without adequate supervision. Johnson *et al.* (1999) also examined to what extent corruption is associated with the onset and/or the depth of financial crises,[7] while Wei (2000) finds evidence that corrupt countries tend to depend on large inflows of foreign capital, with a much larger share of bank loans than FDI, and hence a marked vulnerability to financial crisis.[8] Bad governance has also been called upon in analysing Argentina's protracted difficulties in the eve of the 2002 crisis, with regard to the lack of independent judiciaries and widespread corruption. As Miguel Kiguel put it: 'Argentina's biggest problem is institutional and political – not economic. Hence the priority should be restoring stability with public-sector and institutional reform to deal with a complete vacuum of law'.[9] Michalet (1999) concludes that corruption discourages foreign direct investment while precipitating capital flight; he notes: 'One key aspect of the investment climate is the assessment of political stability as well as transparency and efficiency of the legal and judiciary system'.[10]

Corruption and international financial institutions' lending policies

Until the mid-1990s, governance was not at centre-stage of the international financial institutions' (IFI) policy discussion agenda. Environment protection as well as the role of women and the conditions for promoting sustainable development were then on the front burner. In a major 1989 report entitled 'Sustainable Growth with Equity: A Long-term Perspective for Sub-Saharan Africa', the World Bank recognized that a crisis of governance underlies the litany of Africa's development problems, while giving modest attention to combating corruption.[11] Times have changed. At the 1996 Annual Meeting, World Bank President Jim Wolfensohn spoke about 'the cancer of corruption' and its devastating effect on development.[12] At his first Washington press conference, IMF Managing Director, Horst Köhler stressed the IMF's priority to pay the utmost attention to 'the promotion of transparency and accountability' (IMF Survey, 2000b).

The mounting interest in corruption stems from a combination of better information, greater public awareness, and pressure from NGOs, bilateral donors and taxpayers to enhance scrutiny of the use of public funds. In the USA, Capitol Hill challenged the IFIs as throwing taxpayer money at corrupt regimes and as bailing out incompetent governments. Eradicating corruption had to become a necessary criterion for determining eligibility access to public aid money. OECD country governments, who are also major shareholders in the IFIs, have recognized that corruption is a transnational phenomenon that requires global coalition-building. As early as 1994, the Organization of American States drew up the 'Inter-American Convention Against Corruption', which requires countries to make it a criminal offence to both solicit and accept bribes.[13] As the Centre for Strategic and International Studies notes: 'Since the end of the Cold War, corruption has emerged on the international agenda as one of the most significant transnational issues of our time.'[14]

In short, the IFIs stress the importance of corruption as one of the biggest obstacles to a country's long-term development. They insist on the need for a credible legal system, transparency in spending public funds, and a stable regulatory framework. These issues constitute the core of the so-called 'second-generation policy reforms' aimed at constituting a set of rules and guidelines conducive to private-sector development based on sound institutions. This new emphasis recognizes that development means economic growth plus those conditions that make it sustainable. These conditions include efficient markets, robust institutions, transparency and good governance. Investigating this issue, Gupta *et al.* (1998) established a strong relationship between corruption on the one hand, and income inequality and poverty on the other hand. Furthermore, they showed that the causality was from corruption to income inequality and poverty.

Klitgaard (1998), Gray and Kaufmann (1998) and Mauro (1998) have highlighted that the World Bank pioneered efforts towards combating corruption in member countries in the mid-1990s. The Bank Institute initiated a Governance Programme to build national integrity systems to fight corruption in 1994, and strengthened its anticorruption measures contained in its procurement guideless[15] in 1997. The Bank's Executive Directors adopted new strategies and guidelines to enhance the Bank's efforts to promote good governance and combat corruption in 1998.[16] In addition, the Bank itself cleaned up inside its own yard; in December 2000, the Bank fired staff for allegedly taking bribes from private companies in exchange for awarding them contracts.[17] The Bank set up an 'Anticorruption Knowledge Centre' as well as a Development Forum discussion on anti-corruption strategies. The Centre focuses on a number of emerging-market countries in Africa, Latin America, Asia and Eastern Europe. All in all, 48 countries are involved in specific anti-corruption and governance measures under the Bank's auspices, with Africa at the centre of the Bank's efforts.

The IMF, not to be left behind, has taken several measures to promote good governance policies in member countries since the second half of the 1990s. Beyond morality considerations, the IMF gradually admitted that, in the long-term, corruption is not 'efficient' from the standpoint of sustainable growth requirements. Corruption goes with a malfunctioning government, and this can harm economic performance severely. A few weeks before retiring from the Fund,

Michel Camdessus, former IMF Managing Director, summarized the Fund's position by these words: 'Satisfactory development is not possible when corruption is rampant.'[18] At the September 1996 Interim Committee Meeting, the IMF stressed the importance of sound governance, including transparency, the rule of law, public-sector efficiency and anti-corruption measures.[19] In mid-1997, the IMF enacted a number of 'good public management' principles that constitute the basis of the Fund's surveillance mandate. In addition, the IMF made strides in improving its own governance, particularly through increased openness and transparency (IMF Survey, 2000). The underlying assumption is that market-based economic policies, coupled with privatization and deregulation, reduce the incentive for bribery since state intervention produces loopholes and client–patron relationships; hence a renewed emphasis on private-sector-led growth, so as to minimize state interference with market forces. All in all, poor governance comes with excessive and arbitrary government intervention, discretionary decision-making, lack of transparency, poor management, and an ill-defined regulatory framework.

Corruption and country-risk assessment

It is one thing to claim that corruption is a risk factor along with inflation, deficits and over-indebtedness. Measuring corruption in order to rank countries and to incorporate governance criteria in credit decisions is a more formidable challenge. By definition, it is difficult to use quantitative measurements for illicit practices. Most techniques attempt to capture the degree of corruption in a country through the perceptions of investors, creditors and local economic agents. Polls and panel interviews constitute the main approach, along with the Delphi technique based on a survey of country specialists' opinions. The measure of corruption is thus highly subjective.

One can distinguish four main sources of corruption evaluation; namely, risk-rating agencies, NGOs and academic institutes, specialized private organizations, and the World Bank. Official lenders as well as private investors and creditors can thus use a wide range of corruption measurement sources. There is no deficit of information regarding corruption and governance for country-risk analysts and decision-makers, and the tables that follow capture the salient features of the 15 most useful sources, listed in Table 5.1.

Table 5.1   List of country-risk analysts

- **Business Environment Risk Intelligence** (BERI) provides a political risk index assessing the social and political environment of a country. It is built on the opinion and scores provided by a hundred experts with a diplomatic or political science background. Governance quality is included into political risk analysis along with government effectiveness and social indicators. http://www.beri.com

- The London-based **Economist Intelligence Unit** (EIU) provides a comprehensive country-risk analysis forecast on some 100 EMCs, on a quarterly basis. The EIU method flows from experts' answers to a series of 77 predetermined qualitative and quantitative questions. http://www.eiu.com

- **Euromoney** publishes ratings of some 180 countries since 1982 on a semi-annual basis. The methodology is built from a blend of quantitative criteria and qualitative factors coming from surveys with about 40 political work analysts and economists. Political risk receives a 25% weighting, as much as economic performance. Countries are graded on a scale from 0 (worst) to 100 (best). www.euromoney.com

- **Political Risk Service's** risk analyses cover a hundred countries and are updated on a quarterly basis. The International Country Risk Guide measures and tracks corruption perception in government, law and order, expropriation risk, as well as the quality of bureaucracy. These measures stem from the subjective assessment of experts around the world. http://www.prsgroup.com

- To look upon governance and corruption, **Moody's** takes into consideration the structures of social interaction, social and political dynamics, as well as economic fundamentals. Moody's relies on the judgement of a group of credit-risk professionals to weigh the various risk factors as well as the impact of each of these factors upon business prospects. http://www.moodys.com

- **Institutional Investor's** ratings are published twice a year since 1979 to assess the creditworthiness of about 150 countries, based on a survey of some 100 international bankers' perception of creditworthiness, including economic, financial and sociopolitical stability criteria. The resulting score scales from zero (very high chance of default) to 100 (least chance of default). www.institutionalinvestor.com

- **The World Bank**. Given its unique policy dialogue with more than 180 countries, the World Bank has developed a comprehensive database of composite governance indicators, measuring perceptions of voice and accountability, political stability, government effectiveness, regulatory quality, rule of law, and corruption. www.worldbank.org/wbi/governance/

- **Standard and Poor's** rating approach is both quantitative and qualitative. It is based on a checklist of 10 categories, including governance and political risk. The political risk factors gauge the impact of politics on economic conditions, as well as the quality of governance and the degree of government support in the population. S&P assigns short term and long-term ratings. http://www.standardandpoors.com

- **Transparency International**, a non-profit NGO in Berlin, provides an annual survey of corruption practices in nearly 90 countries since 1995. Their corruption perception index is based on a wide network of information sources with local NGOs, domestic and foreign corporations, investors and business contacts. www.transparency.org

Continued

Table 5.1   Continued

- **Heritage Foundation,** established since 1985 in partnership with the *Wall Street Journal* (WSJ), publishes an economic freedom index for some 160 countries, both industrialized and developing. The ranking is based on 10 sociopolitical and economic criteria, including political stability, state interference, investment codes, regulatory framework, institutional strength, and corruption scope. www.heritage.org

- **Freedom House** since 1972 monitors the progress and decline of political rights and civil liberties in 192 countries, publishing an annual survey of the Progress of Freedom in the world. The ranking is based on a wide survey of regional experts, consultants, and human rights specialists. Political stability and civil liberties are ranked on a scale of 1 (best) to 7 (worst). www.freedomhouse. org/ratings/index.htm

- **PriceWaterhouse Coopers'** opacity index measures the lack of clear, accurate, formal and widely accepted practices in a country's business environment. As such, it focuses on the relative state of corrupt business practices, the transparency of the legal system and the quality of the regulatory framework. It measures the resulting extra risk premium that stems from additional business and economic costs. www.opacityindex.com/

- The political and economic stability index of **Lehman Brothers and Eurasia** measures relative stability in around 20 EMCs by integrating political science theories with financial market developments. The monthly evaluation uses both quantitative and qualitative criteria, including institutional efficiency, political legitimacy, economic performance, and government effectiveness. www.legsi.com

- **The Institute for Management Development's** World Competitiveness Report analyses 49 industrialized and emerging economies around the world based on a far-reaching survey since 1989. Its analysis of the institutional framework addresses issues such as state efficiency, transparency of governmentpolicy, the public service's independence from political interference, bureaucracy as well as bribery and corruption. www.imd.ch

- **Political and Economic Risk Consultancy** (PERC) specializes in strategic business information and analysis in East and Southeast Asia, with an emphasis on corruption and business costs. Annual risk reports survey over 1,000 senior expatriates to obtain their perceptions of corruption, labour quality, intellectual property rights risks and other systemic shortcomings. www.asiarisk.com

Corruption, governance and capital flows

As a measure of corruption, we use the corruption index released by the International Country Risk Index Guide (ICRG), together with the corruption perception indices of Germany-based NGO Transparency International.[20] To measure the broader governance, we use the index of political rights and civil liberties of Freedom House. The secondary market discounts come from Bloomberg's database and the FP Consult database (now part of Fortis Investment Management[21]). Economic data come from the IMF's International Financial Statistics and the World Bank's Global Development Finance database. The sample pools a cross-section of 103 countries, with four sub-periods over the years 1984–2001.

In view of the IFIs' impressive statements against corruption, the quality of governance should be at the forefront of the IFIs' criteria to allocate official funds, including for debt reduction. And, if so, governance performance should further improve following access to debt-relief operations if the latter are predicated on *ex ante* conditions of transparency improvement, and on *ex post* allocation of debt-relief proceeds to priority social needs. This remains to be confirmed.

Corruption and debt-relief eligibility

Official debt relief is widely criticized on two grounds. First, there is not enough aid for pulling developing countries out of the poverty trap. Cohen (2000) criticized the Debt Initiative as lacking a market perspective, thereby not reflecting the actual 'market value' of the debt which should take account of the risk of non-payment. Second, the Initiative has been under US Congress fire for doing too much, i.e. using taxpayer money for subsidizing developing countries' inefficient public management.

A precondition for *ex ante* eligibility to official debt reduction is robust macroeconomic adjustment and strong governance. As former US Treasury Secretary Larry Summers summarizes: 'The highly indebted poor countries (HIPC) debt reduction initiative (adopted in the fall of 1996) is a special effort aimed at promoting mutually reinforcing objectives – poverty reduction, sustainable development, and good governance – while strengthening the incentives for reform and growth.' The HIPC batch should all be members of an 'excellence class', sharing sustained institutionalization efforts, robust macroeconomic frameworks, and good governance. One should expect, thus, that only 'deserving' countries obtain access to donor funds for debt reduction. Many of the debtor countries that are eligible to the HIPC Initiative, however, exemplified both poor macroeconomic performance and bad governance at the time of their access to officially sponsored debt reduction operations. Likewise, Chancellor Brown's debt-cancellation proposal at the G7 meeting in June 2005 includes several countries among the 18 target countries that exemplify dreadful governance records. The deal is to provide prompt and massive relief to such countries as Bolivia, Honduras, Ethiopia and Zambia that all share low levels of corruption perception indices, as reported by Transparency International.

Figure 5.1 illustrates the relationship between country access to official debt reduction and corruption. It shows that beneficiaries of

79

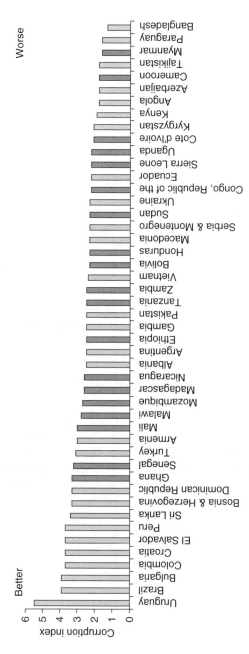

Figure 5.1 Countries eligible to debt-relief programme (in black) and corruption levels as of end-2003

the HIPC initiative are smoothly distributed along the corruption index. Notoriously corrupted countries (to the right of the graph) get similar access to debt-reduction schemes as countries with better corruption records (the latter measured by Transparency International's corruption perception index as of 2003). The initiative seems to lack a 'pro-governance bias'.

Corruption and access to IMF lending

Where does IMF lending go? As of the end of 2003, 55 countries had lending arrangements with the Fund, amounting to some US$83 billion of agreed available resources. What is the relationship between access to IMF lending and corruption? Figure 5.2 illustrates this relationship, between corruption and access to IMF resources at the end of 2003. It clearly shows that IMF resources are equally distributed whatever the corruption level. Countries as notoriously corrupt as Cameroon, Côte d'Ivoire and Bangladesh get access to as many resources as countries like Bulgaria, Croatia, Bosnia, Armenia and Senegal which exemplify robust governance efforts. Given that quotas constitute the leverage for access to IMF resources, our analysis will be refined in a subsequent part of this chapter to take account of the size of the economy in the relationship between corruption and IMF lending flows over a 16-year period.

A dynamic approach to corruption, governance and capital flows

On the face value of our discussion so far, one could expect that: *Other things being equal, low corruption is associated with high official fund allocation.* Based on the mounting attention devoted to corruption by risk-rating agencies, one could also expect that: (1) *Other things being equal, high corruption is associated with low secondary market debt price,* and (2) *High corruption is associated with low private fund allocation.*

To test the hypothesis 'lower corruption/larger capital flows', we use a number of variables including aggregate net resources combining all capital flows, both private and official, before breaking down the sources between three categories of creditors:

- official creditors (bilateral and multilateral);
- private creditors (international banks and bondholders); and
- private investors (FDI and portfolio equity flows).

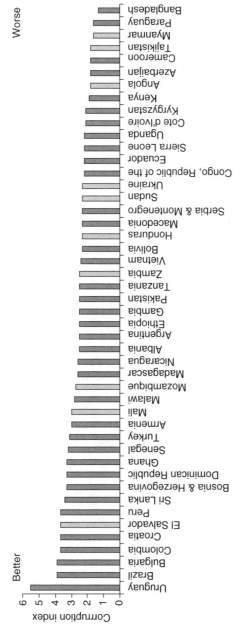

Figure 5.2 Countries with access to IMF lending and corruption levels as of end-2003

The various regressions between corruption and capital flows include two other controlling variables, namely GDP per capita and nominal GNP. The former is a proxy representing the level of economic development, and can possibly have an influence on the amount of capital inflows. Nominal GNP is used to take into account the size of the economy and the quota-based access to IMF resources. As expected, the size of the economy represented by GNP gets a significant positive coefficient. We regress both on panel data over the time period 1984–2001 and on a cross-section basis, with four sub-periods: 1984–2001, 1984–89, 1990–95 and 1996–2001. This choice is not arbitrary: 1984–89 corresponds to the end of the Soviet Union era and the beginning of the official treatment of the debt crisis; 1990–95 corresponds to the emancipation of the Soviet satellites and the EMCs' return to the capital markets; and 1996–2001 coincides with the new IFIs' stance against corruption in a context of acute emerging-market crises (Mexico 1994–95; Asia 1997; Russia 1998; Argentina 2001). Table 5.2 summarizes the main results.

These results cast light on the direction of capital flows according to different categories of creditors, but also on the relative weight of corruption and governance criteria in risk-taking decision-making. Regarding aggregate net resource flows, we find a negative correlation between corruption and capital flows; namely, countries with better control of corruption managed to attract larger external resources, whatever the capital origins. Official flows tend to be associated altogether with lower corruption and better governance.

Regarding FDI flows, clearly, corruption is not a driving variable for investment decision discrimination. Two explanations can be provided. First, corruption tends to 'grease the wheels' as Huntington (1968) suggested. Second, as emerging markets have become all the rage, investors allocate their capital gradually to worse-governance countries, a shortsighted strategy that might lead to signs of an investment bubble should market conditions tighten. As the head of emerging markets at Pictet, the Swiss private bank, concludes regarding Russia and China: 'We are seeing massive oversubscriptions for new listings and valuations that make very little sense. People are buying into the concept of emerging markets without looking too carefully at the details.'[23] Both China and Russia suffer from the worst PricewaterhouseCoopers opacity indices, measuring corruption and legal opacity, while enjoying A2 and Baa3 sovereign ratings from Moody's

Table 5.2 Regression results between corruption, governance and external capital flows

Type of investor	Corruption	Freedom and democracy
Net aggregate resource flows	Lower corruption/ larger net resources	More freedom/ larger capital flows only since 1996
Official flows	Lower corruption/ larger net resources	No relationship
Banks and bondholders	At best no relationship; at worst (1996–2001 period) higher corruption/larger capital flows	Less freedom/larger capital flows
Secondary market discount of London club debt	Higher corruption/ lower debt prices	n/a
Portfolio equity investors	Lower corruption/ larger equity flows	No relationship
FDI	No relationship	More freedom/ larger capital flows

Investors Service, respectively. Regarding private bank lending, we first observe the correlation between corruption and the secondary market price of London Club debt. Market trading volumes, which had grown rapidly in the 1990s, peaked at US$6 trillion in 1997 and then fell off sharply after the Russian default in mid-1998, as investors reevaluated the volatility and returns on emerging-market investments. In 2003, market trading turnover reached about US$3 trillion and liquidity remains high. The discount on debt paper, which is the inverse of the price, reflects both overall market conditions and country-risk assessment. We find a strong correlation between corruption and discount that can be explained by the adverse impact of corruption on the quality of public administration, including debt management, hence lower creditworthiness and higher discount. Figure 5.3 illustrates this positive relation.

The analysis of the relation between private creditors and corruption in emerging-market countries is further enhanced by looking at the direction of bank lending and bond investment. Whereas the secondary market discount applied to the stock of London Club

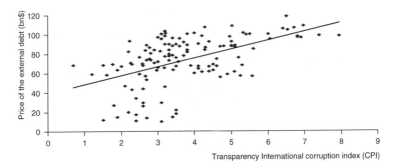

Figure 5.3   Corruption and secondary market discount

exposure, the correlation now explores capital flows from both banks and bondholders, and finds a positive relation between corruption and risk exposure. This is well-illustrated by Venezuela. The country's corruption is ranked 104 by Transparency International, worse than Kazakhstan, Moldova and Uzbekistan, while it successfully reopened market access with a US$1.5 billion seven-year bond deal in mid-2003. The bond enjoyed the 'Deal of the Year' prize of LatinFinance, because 'it raised money cheaply for the government, retired Brady bonds, soaked up surging local currency liquidity and provided access to dollars legally for banks and businesses'.[24]

Why such creditor myopia? A first explanation stems from competition among private lenders and declining spreads, encouraging developing-country borrowers to turn to capital markets. Spreads were historically low in the mid-1990s, just before the Asian crisis, and they fell again in 2003 due to high liquidity and few attractive alternatives. Latin American borrowers, thus, were able to raise close to US$39 billion from international investors in 2003, mostly with low-cost, dollar-denominated debt. Brazil's US$1 billion global bond in April 2003 was a roaring success according to *LatinFinance*. In addition, even though private creditors might incorporate corruption and governance factors in their assessment of country creditworthiness, this does not necessarily translate into declining risk exposure given the huge backlog resulting from the loans made in the previous decades. Today's size of loan and bond portfolios is the consequence of yesterday's exposure policy. Indeed, the 1980s and most of the early

1990s have been marked by concerted and 'defensive' lending operations, initially under the Baker refinancing plan, and later under debt exchange offers coupled with the retirement of Brady bonds.

Conclusions

This chapter has tackled the issue of governance and corruption from the standpoint of two categories of foreign creditors, namely official institutions and private capital markets. Corruption is the symptom of deeply-rooted institutional weaknesses in a country's economy. At the root of corruption, a kleptocratic state manages to parasite the country's economy. Nepotism, in turn, increases distortions in resource allocation and exacerbates income inequalities. At minimum, corruption discourages domestic savings and investment due to its tax effect. At worst, it triggers capital flight and brain drain.

Whereas the political economy literature considers corruption as a fatality or a sort of 'natural disaster' that stems from the very process of institutional modernization, the economics literature analyses it as rent-seeking behaviour. All this is of little comfort for creditors and investors. We have examined how much governance is incorporated in lending decisions by official institutions and by private lenders, showing that, whatever the bells and whistles, IFIs tend to allocate public money particularly for debt-reduction programmes, without drastic discrimination with respect to corrupt regimes. Their lending record, however, suggests that IFIs lend more to less corrupt and more democratic countries. This is in echo, with important nuances, of Alesina and Weder (1999) who showed that there is no evidence that bilateral or multilateral aid goes disproportionately to less corrupt governments. In fact, if anything, they find the opposite: 'more corrupt governments receive more foreign aid than less corrupt ones'.[25] Our results show, however, a marked correlation between government loans and corrupt regimes. Bilateral creditors, clearly, tend to allocate more funds to more corrupt and less democratic countries. Regarding private investors, including banks, bondholders and equity investors, corruption and governance are not driving criteria for risk-exposure strategy decisions. There is thus a wide gap between better information regarding corruption and governance for country-risk assessment, and incorporating these criteria into decision-making.

Notes

1. For an illustration of 'Dutch disease', see Brian Pinto (1987), 'Nigeria During and After the Oil Boom: A Policy Comparison with Indonesia', *The World Bank Economic Review*, vol. 1(3) (May), pp. 419–45.
2. World Bank (1989), 'Sustainable Growth with Equity: A Long-Term Perspective for Sub-Saharan Africa', Report no. 8014 (15 August), p. 59.
3. D. Kaufman, A. Kraay and P. Zoido-Lobatao (2000), 'Gestion des Affaires Publiques', *Finance and Development*, vol. 37(2) (June), p. 10.
4. See for instance Bardhan (1997).
5. Samuel P. Huntington (1969), *Political Order in Changing Societies* (New Haven and London: Yale University Press), p. 69.
6. See Andre Gunder Frank (1980), *Crisis in the World Economy* (New York: Holmes & Meier), pp. 320–2.
7. Simone Johnson, Peter Boone, Alasdair Breach and Eric Friedman (2000), 'Corporate Governance in the Asian Financial Crisis', *Journal of Financial Economics*, vol. 58(1–2), pp. 141–86.
8. Shang-Jin Wei (2000), 'Negative Alchemy? Corruption, Composition of Capital Flows, and Currency Crises', draft paper, Brookings Institution, 11 December.
9. 'Peru's Leader Calls on World to Provide Aid for Argentina', *Financial Times*, 5 February 2002, p. 8.
10. Charles-Albert Michalet (1999), 'La Séduction des Nations', *Economica*, p. 73.
11. World Bank (1989) 'Sustainable Growth with Equity: A Long-Term Perspective for Sub-Saharan Africa', Report no. 8014 (15 August) (see pp. 59–60).
12. See: 'Preventing Corruption in Bank Projects', World Bank's Anti-corruption Knowledge Center, home page www1.worldbank.org/publicsector/anticorrupt/prevent.htm
13. As a matter of fact, only 20 out of 34 OAS member states have ratified the agreement.
14. 'Turkish Economy Shaken by Corruption Revelations', World Bank Press Review, 15 January 2001, p. 8.
15. *World Bank Annual Report* (1997), pp. 4–5. The *Report* index contains five references to corruption.
16. *World Bank Annual Report* (1998), p. 11. The *Report* index contains six references to corruption.
17. World Bank spokesman Caroline Anstey, World Bank Press Review, 7 December 2000.
18. 'Capacity Building, Governance, and Economic Reform in Africa', 2 November 1999. Inaugural Seminar of the Joint Africa Institute.
19. *Rapport Annuel du FMI*, 1998, chapter 6, Surveillance, p. 42.
20. This database can be downloaded at http://www.transparency.de/ or at http://www.gwdg.de/~uwvw/
21. Thanks to Didier Lambert from Fortis Investment Management for help in collecting the data.

22. Statement to the Development Committee, 17 April 2000.
23. Portfolio: 'Pictet takes a long-term look at emerging markets', *Financial Times*, Fund Management, February 2004, p. 5.
24. *LatinFinance*, no. 204, February 2004, p. 33.
25. A. Alesina and B. Weder (1999), 'Do Corrupt Governments Receive Less Foreign Aid?', National Bureau of Economic Research, Working Paper no. 7108 (May), p. 4.

References

Bardhan, P. (1997) 'Corruption and Development: A Review of Issues', *Journal of Economic Literature* (September), vol. xxxv, p. 1321.
Beck, P.J. and Maher, M.W. (1986), 'A Comparison of Bribery and Bidding in Thin Markets', *Economic Letters*, vol. 20, pp. 1–5.
Bouchet, M., Clark, E. and Groslambert, B. (2003) *Country Risk Assessment* (London: Wiley).
Charap, J. and Harm, C. (1999) 'Institutionalized Corruption and the Kleptocratic State', IMF Working Paper no. 99/91-EA (July).
Cohen, D. (2000) 'The HIPC Initiative: True and False Promises', ENS and OECD Development Centre (August).
Gamer, R.E. (1976) *The Developing Nations: A Comparative Perspective* (Boston: Allyn and Bacon).
Gray, C. and Kaufmann, D. (1998) 'Corruption and Development', *Finance and Development* (March), vol. 35(1), pp. 7–10.
Gupta, S., Davoodi, H. and Alonso-Terme, R. (1998) 'Does Corruption Affect Income Inequality and Poverty', IMF Working Paper no. WP/98/76.
Harberger, A.C. (1988) 'Policymaking and Economic Policy in Small Developing Countries', in R. Dornbusch and L. Helmers (eds) *The Open Economy*, Dornbusch, EDI Series in Economic Development, pp. 249–63 (Oxford: Oxford University Press).
Hines J. (1995) 'Forbidden Payment: Foreign Bribery and American Business After 1977', National Bureau of Economic Research Working Paper no. 5266 (September).
Huntington, S.P. (1968) *Political Order in Changing Societies* (New Haven and London: Yale University Press).
IMF/World Bank Development Committee (2000), 17 April.
IMF Press Release no. 99/40.
IMF Survey (2000).
Klitgaard, R. (1998) 'International Corruption against Governance', *Finance and Development* (March), vol. 35(1), p. 6.
Krueger, A.O. (1993) 'Virtuous and Vicious Circles in Economic Development', *American Economic Review*, vol. 83(2), pp. 351–5.
Krugman, P. (1979) 'A Model of Balance-of-Payments Crises', *Journal of Money, Credit, and Banking*, vol. 11, pp. 311–25.

Krugman, P. (1994) 'The Myth of Asia's Miracle', *Foreign Affairs* (November).

Krugman, P. (1998a) *'What Happened to Asia'* (January), mimeo.

Krugman, P. (1998b) *Will Asia Bounce Back*? Speech for Credit Swiss First Boston, Hong Kong (March), pp. 1–7.

Krugman, P. (1999) *Balance Sheets, the Transfer Problem, and Financial Crises* (January), mimeo prepared for the festschrift volume in honour of Robert Flood, also downloadable on http://web.mit.edu/krugman/www/flood.pdf

LatinFinance (2000) 'Lenders are Leaning on Governments to Clean up Corruption' (September), p. 54.

Leff, N.H. (1964) 'Economic Development through Bureaucratic Corruption', *The American Behavioral Scientist*, vol. 8(2), pp. 8–14.

Leite, C. and Weidmann, J. (1999) 'Does Mother Nature Corrupt: Natural Resources, Corruption and Economic Growth', IMF Working Paper no. WP/99/85, (July).

Lien, D.H. (1986) 'Notes on Competitive Bribery Games', *Economic Letters*, vol. 22, pp. 337–41.

Lui, F.T. (1985) 'Equilibrium Queuing Model of Bribery', *Journal of Political Economy*, vol. 93(4), pp. 760–81.

Mauro, P. (1995) 'Corruption and Growth', *Quarterly Journal of Economics* (August), pp. 681–711.

Mauro, P. (1998) 'Corruption: Causes, Consequences, and the Way Forward', *Finance and Development* (March), vol. 35(1), pp. 11–14.

Michalet, C.A. (1999) 'La Séduction des Nations', *Economica*, p. 73.

Murphy, K.M., Shleifer, A. and Vishny, R.W. (1991) 'The Allocation of Talent: Implications for Growth', *Quarterly Journal of Economics* (May), pp. 503–30.

Nye, J. (1967) 'Corruption and Political Development: A Cost–Benefit Analysis', *American Political Science Review*, vol. 61, pp. 417–27.

Rose-Ackerman, S. (1975) 'The Economics of Corruption', *Journal of Public Economics*, vol. 4, pp. 187–203.

Rose-Ackerman, S. (1978) *Corruption: A Study in Political Economy* (New York: Academic Press).

Shleifer, A. and Vishny, R.W. (1993) 'Corruption', *Quarterly Journal of Economics*, vol. 108, pp. 599–617.

Tanzi, V. (1998) 'Corruption Around the World', *IMF Staff Papers*, vol. 45 (December).

Wei, S. (1997) 'How Taxing is Corruption on International Investors?', *NBER Working Paper* Series no. 6030, National Bureau of Economic Research.

Young, A. (1995) 'The Tyranny of Numbers: Confronting the Statistical Realities of the East Asian Growth Experience', *Quarterly Journal of Economics* (August), pp. 641–80.

6
Market Deregulations, Volatility and Spillover Effects: Experiences from Emerging Stockmarkets

*Duc Khuong Nguyen**

Introduction

The last two decades have been a period of spectacular development in emerging stockmarkets; both the market size and level of sophistication have rapidly increased over time.[1] Most would agree that these developments could not have happened without an intensive course of stockmarket liberalizations undertaken by developing countries in the late 1980s. However, the arrival of 1990s' financial turbulences in emerging markets (for example Latin America in 1994; Asia in 1997; Russia in 1998) suggests that market openings might induce financial instability and strengthen the volatility of stockmarkets through causing institutional changes, asset price bubbles and irregular shifts in economic activities. This has led to a vast body of research into the relationship between market liberalization and stockmarket volatility in emerging countries (see for example Bekaert and Harvey, 1997; Kim and Singal, 2000; and Miles, 2002). To date, we recognize, however, that this issue is still under debate.

Recently, several papers have been concerned by the volatility linkages between emerging markets and other markets around the world (for example Liu and Pan, 1997; and He, 2001). Obviously, they are

* CERAG-UMR 5820 CNRS, University of Grenoble II, 150 Rue de la Chimie, BP 47, 38040 Grenoble, France; e-mail: *duc.nguyen@upmf-grenoble.fr.* Tel.: +33 (0)1 40 78 83 83. I am grateful to Professor Patrice Fontaine for his helpful comments and guidance throughout this research.

motivated by the increased integration of these markets with world markets as documented in Bekaert and Harvey (1995), and Carrieri *et al.* (2002). The growing interest on volatility spillover effects can also be explained by the creation of global financial instruments (such as ADRs, and country funds) which are directly associated with emerging-market securities and the instantaneous connection of emerging markets with world marketplaces given the technological advances in telecommunications.

This chapter will contribute to the above literature in the sense that it analyses the induced impact of market deregulations on the conditional variance for six of the largest emerging markets of the world. I also investigate the dynamic linkages of volatility between selected emerging markets and two global markets, the USA and Japan stock-markets, and further examine whether market openings impact this international transmission of volatility.

The study is structured as follows: the next section offers a brief review of the related literature; followed by a description of the data and methodology; a report and interpretation of the obtained empirical results; and finally a discussion of the implications of the empirical results for foreign portfolio investments and asset-pricing formulations in emerging markets.

Related literature

Previous studies are divergent about the impacts of market liberalizations on emerging-market volatility. Theoretically, there are a total of three scenarios. First, market liberalization may drive up stock volatility through the free circulation of capital flows and the speculative positions of foreign investors in domestic markets. Recent crises during the 1990s constitute plausible proofs for such a scenario. Moreover, informational asymmetry between domestic and foreign investors which leads to excessive trading volume may also contribute to a significant increase in domestic market volatility. Second, the view that market liberalization reduces emerging-market volatility is not at all unreasonable. It is widely demonstrated that market openings help to improve informational efficiency of emerging markets by leading to the enhancement of market transparency and liquidity (see for example Levine and Zervos, 1998; Kim and Singal, 2000). Since in efficient capital markets current price becomes the best forecast of share value, there will be only a small number of trades on financial assets. Accordingly, if emerging markets have become more efficient after financial liberalization, stockmarket volatility should decline. Finally, market openings may have insignificant impact on emerging-market volatility because one may expect that liberalization effects in different directions are perfectly compensated.

Empirically, the findings of previous works seem to confirm theoretical anticipations. Bekaert and Harvey (1997), for example, analysed the impact of market openings on conditional volatility in 20 emerging markets and found that, on average, market liberalization does not drive up local market volatility. The analysis of Kim and Singal (2000) indicates that average volatilities of emerging markets are lowered in the post-liberalization period. By contrast, Miles (2002) shows that market opening has a statistically significant impact in almost three-fifths of sample markets, but in most cases the effect of liberalizations is to raise rather than lower the variance of stock returns. There is also empirical evidence to suggest that the impact of market openings on the variability of emerging-market returns is statistically insignificant or even worthless (see De Santis and Imrohoroglu, 1997; and Bekaert and Harvey, 2000). In a related study, Aggarwal *et al.* (1999) note that market liberalization events do not coincide with sudden shifts in emerging-market volatility.

With growing market integration, both researchers and practitioners have switched their attention to the international transmission of volatility across capital markets. However, the emphasis has manifestly been on developed markets (see for example Masulis *et al.*, 1990; Karolyi, 1995; Leachman and Francis, 1996; and Kearney, 2000). For example, Karolyi (1995) explored daily data to evaluate how conditional mean and volatility are transmitted between the USA and Canadian stockmarkets. Using simultaneously multivariate GARCH and vector autoregression (VAR) models, the author observes that shocks from the USA have a larger impact on the variability of non-interlisted stock returns than on the variability of cross-listed stocks. Leachman and Francis (1996) sought to examine the volatility spillover among the G-7 developed countries and found evidence that volatility in each stockmarket is substantially linked to volatility shocks in foreign markets. They also point out that monetary policy coordination marked by the Plaza Accord has substantial impacts on the dynamic transmission of volatility.

A few studies have been concerned with emerging markets. Liu and Pan (1997), for example, studied the volatility spillover effects from the US and Japanese stockmarkets to four Asian markets including Hong Kong, Singapore, Taiwan and Thailand. They found that the Japanese stockmarket exerts a more important impact on the volatilities of Asian markets than the US stockmarkets. In a related study, He (2001) highlights the volatility spillover effects among the US, Hong Kong and South Korean markets. The author shows that South Korea appears to have fewer responses to the return volatility of the US stockmarkets, while the inverse scenario applied to the Hong Kong stockmarket.

In this chapter I propose to enhance the above empirical literature by using a bivariate AR(1,1)-GARCH(1,1)-in-Mean model which controls for both local and global risk premiums related, respectively, to the conditional variance of the local market index and to the conditional covariance between local and world market indices. The importance of this specification is that it ensures the more general dynamics between local and world market volatilities. Volatility spillover effects among sample markets are then examined by using the VAR methodology as in Karolyi (1995). The impact of market liberalizations on emerging-market volatility is carried out by testing the relationships between the fitted volatility series and proxy variables for market liberalization. On the other hand, splitting the study periods into two sub-samples allows us to explore the impact of market liberalization on the spillover effects.

Data and methodology

Sample data

The volatility of sample market and cross-market volatility spillover effects are examined using stockmarket indices on a monthly basis. The population of emerging markets includes Argentina, Brazil, Chile, South Korea, Mexico and Thailand. The global markets are represented by the United States and Japan. The data are Standard and Poor's International Financial Corporation Global (S&P/IFCG) total return indices for emerging markets and Morgan Stanley Capital International Inc. (MSCI) total return indices for two developed markets. The MSCI world index is used as proxy of world markets to estimate our bivariate model for conditional volatility. All the data are expressed in US dollar terms and obtained from Datastream over the period from January 1976 to January 2003.

Monthly returns for each market are calculated by taking the differences in the natural logs of the total return index. Statistical properties of the monthly return series are presented in Table 6.1. The findings are similar to those of previous works and indicate that emerging markets are more volatile than global markets (see Claessens *et al.*, 1995; Harvey, 1995). The high significance of skewness and excess kurtosis coefficients coupled with the significance of the Jarque–Bera statistics demonstrates that return series are not normally distributed, except for Japan. The Ljung–Box test for the cumulative autocorrelation up to 12 lags applied to returns shows evidence of significant linear dependencies in three markets (Chile, Mexico and Thailand). When testing the serial correlation in squared returns, we observe that non-linear dependencies cannot be rejected in six of the sample markets. We also performed the Engle (1982) test to check for the possibility of having conditional heteroscedasticity in return series. The results typically indicate that ARCH effects are present in the return series of most sample markets. Finally, the Augmented Dickey–Fuller test for stationarity indicates that all return series are stationary.

Overall, the diagnostics of monthly data indicate that ARCH effects need to be taken into account in order to capture the leptokurtic distribution and time-varying variances of stock returns.

Table 6.1 Basic statistics for monthly stock returns

	Mean	Std. dev.	Skewness	Kurtosis	Q(12)	Q²(12)	JB	ARCH(4)	ADF
Argentina	1.150	21.884	0.115**	5.401**	10.992	56.320^{++}	395.762^{++}	25.864^{++}	−9.007^{++}
Brazil	0.522	15.795	−0.436**	2.856**	11.002	51.587^{++}	120.845^{++}	7.238	−8.835^{++}
Chile	1.619	9.694	0.334**	2.035**	51.999^{++}	56.726^{++}	62.147^{++}	10.877^{+}	−7.170^{++}
South Korea	0.794	10.731	0.396**	2.846**	8.404	127.652^{++}	118.200^{++}	51.017^{++}	−7.296^{++}
Mexico	0.998	12.924	−2.028**	10.279**	31.962^{++}	36.561^{++}	1653.747^{++}	38.678^{++}	−7.461^{++}
Thailand	0.622	10.348	−0.461**	3.052**	45.377^{++}	186.793^{++}	137.748^{++}	46.609^{++}	−8.454^{++}
United States	0.952	4.463	−0.742*	2.894**	12.011	6.812	143.320^{++}	2.444	−7.291^{++}
Japan	0.709	6.560	0.086	0.493	19.895	31.499^{++}	3.705	10.921^{+}	−6.821^{++}
World	0.868	4.179	−0.679**	1.745**	16.583	9.720	66.294^{++}	1.983	−7.028^{++}

Notes: Sample mean and standard deviations are expressed in percentage terms. Q(12) and Q²(12) are respectively the empirical statistics of the Ljung–Box test for autocorrelation of returns and squared returns up to 12 lags. JB is the Jarque–Bera (1980) test for normal distribution of the return series. ARCH(4) is the chi-squared statistic of Engle's (1982) test for conditional heteroscedasticity using residuals from an AR(1) return-generating process. ADF is the augmented form of the Dickey and Fuller (1981) test for the stationarity of return series. The critical value for the ADF test at 1% is −3.43.
* and ** denote statistical significance at 5% and 1% respectively.
$^{+}$ and $^{++}$ indicate that the null hypotheses of no autocorrelation, normality, conditional homocedasticity and non-stationarity are rejected at the 5% and 1% levels of significance respectively.

Modeling stockmarket volatility and spillover effects

Financially, stockmarket volatility refers to the variability of market index prices, and it can be unconditionally measured by the variance or standard deviation of market index returns. The evidence that stockmarket volatility changes over time suggests the usefulness of conditional volatility. To estimate conditional volatility, some studies have been based on the Schwert (1989) procedure, while others have employed various versions of (generalized) autoregressive conditional heteroscedasticity (ARCH/GARCH) models initially proposed by Engle (1982) and Bollerslev (1986) respectively. A large body of empirical literature (for example Bekaert and Harvey, 1997; Aggarwal *et al.*, 1999; and Kim and Singal, 2000) has pointed out that GARCH-type models successfully characterize stylized empirical regularities of asset returns in emerging markets such as leptokurtic distribution and volatility clustering. Therefore, this study also uses GARCH model for modeling conditional volatility.

Given that stockmarket returns of market *i*, $r_{i,t}$, are generated by an autoregressive process AR(1) as follows:

$$r_{i,t} = \delta_0 + \delta_1 r_{i,t-1} + \varepsilon_{i,t} \tag{6.1}$$

and assuming in addition that return innovations $\varepsilon_{i,t}$ are normally distributed with a mean of zero and a time-varying variance of $h_{i,t}$, a standard GARCH(p,q) can be expressed as:

$$h_{i,t} = \omega + \sum_{j=1}^{p} \alpha_j \varepsilon_{i,t-j}^2 + \sum_{j=1}^{q} \beta_j h_{i,t-j} \tag{6.2}$$

Equation (6.2) suggests that current conditional volatility is a linear function of both the *p* past return innovations and its own *q* lagged conditional. Although we can let the current conditional volatility be dependent on the entire history of past return innovations and conditional volatilities, Bollerslev *et al.* (1992) suggest that a GARCH(1,1) model is quite successful in fitting most of the financial series. Specifically, when examining emerging-market volatility, two concerns must be taken into account. First, there is evidence to suggest that emerging equity markets are not fully segmented from world markets. This implies that domestic market volatility will be affected by world market volatility. A way to achieve this end consists in using a bivariate GARCH(1,1) which allows for both own-market and cross-market dependencies in conditional volatility (see Engle and Kroner, 1995). This specification is advantageous because it guarantees a positive-definite covariance matrix and allows for more general volatility dynamics compared to other alternatives such as Bollerslev's (1990) constant-correlation model. Second, the theory suggests some kinds of relationship between expected returns and risk of financial assets to be guaranteed by financial models. For example, high risk requires high expected returns. To control for this issue, we specify the GARCH-in-mean effects in the return-generating equation as in Bollerslev, Engle and Wooldridge (1988). Finally, it is reasonable to let the conditional covariance between local and world market indices enter the mean equation of the local market since partially integrated markets will be exposed to world market risk. Precisely, our empirical model for stockmarket volatility will be a system of three equations:

$$r_{w,t} = \delta_0 + \delta_1 r_{w,t-1} + \delta_2 h_{w,t} + \varepsilon_{w,t} \tag{6.3}$$

$$r_{i,t} = \lambda_0 + \lambda_1 r_{i,t-1} + \lambda_2 h_{i,t} + \lambda_3 h_{iw,t} + \varepsilon_{i,t} \tag{6.4}$$

$$H_t = C_0'C_0 + A_1'\varepsilon_{t-1}\varepsilon_{t-1}'A_1 + B_1'H_{t-1}B_1 \tag{6.5}$$

where $\varepsilon_t = [\varepsilon_{w,t}, \varepsilon_{i,t}]'$, and $\varepsilon_t \sim N(0, H_t)$. Equations (6.3) and (6.4) correspond to return generating processes of world and local markets respectively. Equation (6.5) refers to the conditional volatility process. C_0, A_1 and B_1 are (2×2) parameter matrices with C_0 upper-triangular. $h_{w,t}$ and $h_{i,t}$, respectively the conditional variance of world and local market indices, correspond to the first and second elements in the diagonal of H_t. $h_{iw,t}$ is the element below the diagonal of H_t, expressing the conditional covariance between local and world markets. The coefficients associated with the conditional variance and covariance will have the interpretation of the time-varying local and global risk premiums respectively.

To investigate the dynamic relationship of conditional volatilities between the stockmarkets, we apply the VAR methodology as in Karolyi (1995) because it permits us to handle the mutual effects among sample markets and the part of domestic market volatility that can be attributable to other markets in the system. In a standard form, a VAR model of order p can be represented by:

$$Y_t = c + \beta_1 Y_{t-1} + \beta_2 Y_{t-2} + \cdots + \beta_p Y_{t-p} + u_t$$

$$= c + \sum_{s=1}^{p} B_s Y_{t-s} + u_t \qquad (6.6)$$

where $Y_t = (Y_{1t}, Y_{2t}, ..., Y_{nt})$ is a $(n \times 1)$ vector of endogenous variables; B_s's are $(n \times n)$ matrices of coefficients; c is a $(n \times 1)$ vector of constants; p is the optimal number of lags; and $u_t = (u_{1t}, u_{2t}, ..., u_{nt})$ is a $(n \times 1)$ vector of uncorrelated white noise having positive definite covariance matrix $\sum = E(u_t u_t')$.

Like a univarite autoregression model having a moving average representation, a VAR model can also be written as a vector moving average (VMA) representation. That is, endogenous variables of the VAR model are expressed in term of current and past values of shocks or innovations in each equation (that is, $u_{1t}, u_{2t}, ..., u_{nt}$):

$$Y_t = C_t\theta + \sum_{s=0}^{\infty} \Phi_s u_{t-s} \qquad (6.7)$$

where $C_t\theta$ represents the deterministic part of Y_t. The i,jth coefficient of Φ_s indicates the effect of a one-unit shock in the jth variable on the ith variable of Y_t after s periods. For example, the instantaneous impact of a one-unit shock to Y_{2t} on Y_{1t} is $\Phi_{12}(0)$. After one period, this effect will be $\Phi_{12}(1)$. To obtain the effects of a particular shock to one of the system innovations on the values of the endogenous variables, we need to orthogonalize the innovations in equation (6.7) so that they are not correlated. Given that volatility links over sample markets are not governed by any explicit economic theory, the Choleski factorization can be straightforwardly used to get uncorrelated innovations. In this way, equation (6.7) can be written in the following form (see Enders, 1995):

$$Y_t = C_t\theta + \sum_{s=0}^{\infty} \Theta_s v_{t-s} \qquad (6.8)$$

where $\Theta_s = \Phi_s G$ and $v_t = G^{-1} u_t$ which satisfy $E(v_t v_t') = I$, i.e., the covariance matrix of the new innovations is an identity matrix.

Accordingly, $\Theta(s)$ contains the impulse response functions of all endogenous variables when the system is shocked by one variable. It is convenient to note that, from the above equation, we can make further explorations about the dynamic interrelations among the variables in the system through computing the variance decomposition. The idea is that the movement of a variable in k-step-ahead forecast horizons can be decomposed into its own shocks and shocks to the other variables.

In our analysis, endogenous variables Y_t are monthly stockmarket volatilities of sample markets which obtained from estimating the bivariate AR(1)-GARCH(1,1) model. Thereby, n is set to be equal to eight. Under the VAR setting, the mechanism of volatility transmission among markets is effectuated through the presence of past realizations of conditional volatility of all markets in the volatility equation of one particular market.

Estimation issues

To obtain the conditional volatility for individual markets included in the sample, we proceed in two steps. First, we estimate the conditional volatility of the world market using equation (6.3) and a univariate GARCH(1,1) as in equation (6.2), and save the results. Second, the system of equations from (6.3) to (6.5) is simultaneously estimated for each of eight markets in the sample imposing the estimated parameters in the first step. This allows us to keep the world market risk to be the same for all markets.[2] The estimation of model parameters is fulfilled by the method of quasi-maximum likelihood estimation (QMLE) proposed by Bollerslev and Wooldridge (1992). The optimization strategy is based on the Broyden–Fletcher–Goldfarb–Shanno (BFGS) algorithm.

The estimated series of conditional volatility for eight markets will serve as inputs for the VAR model. We rely on information criteria such as the Akaike information criterion (AIC) and the Bayesian information criterion (BIC) to determine the optimal number of lags for the VAR model since it is naturally unknown. Accordingly, both the AIC and BIC criteria select the 3-lag model which implies that p is set to three. Hence, the total of free coefficients to be estimated is equal to 200. Since all volatility series are stationary (cf. Table 6.3), we can estimate the VAR(3) using OLS method.

Empirical results

Dynamics of conditional volatility

Table 6.2 reports the estimation results for the conditional variance of the MSCI world index. Panel A provides evidence of the absence of relationships between risk and returns in the world market index since the 'in-mean' parameter is statistically insignificant. It is important to note that the volatility of the world market index tends to be persistent over time as β is very high and strongly significant. Panels B and C summarize statistics for conditional volatility series and diagnostics of standardized residuals. Note that the results from the Ljung–Box Q-statistic also allow us to claim the persistence of volatility.

Table 6.3 illustrates estimated parameters and gives a detailed diagnostic of the estimates of stockmarket volatility for eight individual markets in the sample and standardized residuals. Panel A indicates

Table 6.2 Estimation results of world market volatility

Panel A: estimated coefficients						
δ_0 $(\times 10^2)$	δ_1 $(\times 10^2)$	δ_2	ω $(\times 10^2)$	α	β	*Log-likelihood*
0.833	0.655	0.033	0.008	0.048	0.908**	−868.337
(1.22)	(6.637)	(6.989)	(0.008)	(0.034)	(0.071)	

Panel B: summary statistics for volatility series						
Mean $(\times 10^2)$	*Std. dev.* $(\times 10^2)$	*Minimum* $(\times 10^2)$	*Maximum* $(\times 10^2)$	*Skewness*	*Kurtosis*	*Q(12)*
0.178	0.044	0.011	0.353	1.073	1.191	1665.857++

Panel C: diagnostics of standardized residuals						
Mean	*Std. dev.*	*Skewness*	*Kurtosis*	*Q(12)*	*$Q^2(12)$*	*ARCH(4)*
0.003	0.992	−0.767**	1.882**	16.661	6.196	1.458

Notes: Panel A contains estimated coefficients for conditional mean and variance equations. Bollerslev and Wooldridge's (1992) robust standard errors for non-normality are given in parentheses. Panels B and C report summary statistics for conditional volatility series and diagnostics of standardized residuals. Please refer to notes to Table 6.1 for statistical test specifications.
* and ** denote statistical significance at 5% and 1% levels respectively.
+ and ++ indicate that the null hypotheses of statistical tests are rejected at the 5% and 1% levels of significance respectively.

that most of the risk-premium parameters related to both conditional variance of local markets and conditional covariance between local and world markets are negative and statistically insignificant. There is only a little evidence of a significant impact of conditional covariance on local market returns at the 5 per cent level in Brazil, but the negative sign of the associated coefficient is difficult to interpret.[3] Though estimated coefficients of the bivariate GARCH(1,1) are highly significant, they are not reported here due to space constraints. They are, however, available on request from the author.

Panel B of Table 6.3 provides summary statistics for monthly stock-market volatilities. It appears that the stockmarkets of Argentina and Brazil are the most volatile over the estimation period, followed by Mexico, Thailand, South Korea and Chile. It is interesting to remark that on a monthly basis the level of return variability in the less-volatile emerging market (that is, Chile) is about six times the volatility of the US stockmarket and more than twice that of the Japanese stockmarket. In addition, the Ljung–Box statistic test of order twelve supports the hypothesis of linear dependency in all volatility series, and thus indicates the time-varying persistence of volatility. The stationarity of volatility indices is also examined by the ADF test with intercept and four supplementary lags. The results do not permit us to reject the hypothesis of stationary series.

Figure 6.1 depicts the time paths of monthly conditional volatility series. This graph shows that, except for the last three months of 1987, stockmarkets in the sample were not so volatile during the 1980s. Markets which were most respondent to the market crash of October 1987 include the stockmarkets of the USA, Japan, Thailand, Mexico and Brazil. For example, the typical value of the US conditional variance in November 1987 was about 3.25 per cent compared to the mean of only 0.2 per cent per month. In the case of the Thai stockmarket, these values were 5.42 per cent and 1.5 per cent respectively.

The Latin American debt crisis of 1982–83 does not seem to have generated extreme volatility for emerging markets in the region. The volatility of stockmarkets in Thailand and South Korea, while appearing to be less affected by the Latin American crisis, was remarkably raised during the Asian financial crisis. Apart from some periods of financial turbulence such as the ones mentioned above, we found that the increase of stockmarket volatility seems to be associated with country-specific events. Argentina is an interesting case. Indeed, the volatility of this stockmarket seems to correspond with financial

Table 6.3 Conditional volatility of sample stockmarkets

	Argentina	Brazil	Chile	South Korea	Mexico	Thailand	United States	Japan
				Panel A: estimated parameters				
λ_0	0.008	−0.0247	0.069	0.009	0.062	0.015	0.014**	0.015
	(0.015)	(0.029)	(0.096)	(0.006)	(0.047)	(0.014)	(0.003)	(0.017)
λ_1	0.019	0.106	0.244**	0.105	0.206**	0.314**	−0.036	0.058
	(0.085)	(0.056)	(0.050)	(0.057)	(0.043)	(0.058)	(0.031)	(0.040)
λ_2	0.314	−6.199*	3.205	0.641	6.015	−1.895	1.825	3.048
	(1.787)	(2.607)	(7.998)	(1.210)	(6.502)	(2.701)	(3.110)	(7.444)
λ_3	−0.135	1.648	−5.914	−0.426	−4.406	−0.907	−2.280	−3.220
	(0.387)	(1.201)	(10.408)	(0.730)	(3.831)	(1.522)	(3.253)	(7.286)
Log-likelihood	1157.02	1292.15	1431.33	1436.99	1374.59	1445.83	1901.43	1668.24
			Panel B: statistics for monthly stockmarket volatility series					
Mean	0.077	0.035	0.012	0.014	0.019	0.015	0.002	0.005
Std. dev.	0.083	0.023	0.003	0.009	0.007	0.015	0.002	0.003
Min.[a]	0.122	0.140	0.092	0.058	0.124	0.056	0.010	0.023
Max.[a]	5.709	1.764	0.373	0.715	0.698	1.166	0.325	0.249
Skewness	3.418**	3.102**	3.827**	2.893**	3.111**	3.460**	6.687**	2.760**

Kurtosis	14.054**	12.817**	22.326**	11.410**	14.406**	14.525**	70.974**	10.733**
Q(12)	302.024++	208.637++	29.283++	301.726++	85.544++	671.719++	88.354++	282.223++
ADF(4)	-5.355++	-4.896++	-6.019++	-5.156++	-6.668++	-3.593++	-5.824++	-4.462++

Panel C: diagnostics of standardized residuals

Mean[b]	0.855	-0.030	-0.013	-0.059	-0.142	0.136	0.934	0.444
Std. dev.	0.193	0.238	0.388	0.372	0.315	0.391	0.879	0.616
Skewness	-0.584**	-0.795**	-0.665**	-0.709**	-0.763**	-0.393**	-0.685**	-0.661**
Kurtosis	2.916**	2.449**	1.777**	2.343**	2.143**	1.228**	2.300**	2.184**
Q(12)	12.033	16.191	15.931	12.766	15.046	18.571	13.589	14.432
Q^2(12)	21.107+	14.431	18.229	9.178	8.227	20.306	55.640	19.720
JB	128.909++	111.586++	64.538++	103.703++	90.574++	27.837++	93.663++	85.230++
ARCH(4)	1.089	2.226	1.915	0.905	2.362	0.569	1.723	2.391

Notes: Panel A contains estimated coefficients of the conditional mean equation and maximum values of log-likelihood functions. Bollerslev and Wooldridge's (1992) robust standard errors for non-normality are given in parentheses. Panels B and C provide summary statistics for conditional volatility series and diagnostics of standardized residuals. See also notes to Table 6.1 for statistical test specifications.

* and ** denote statistical significance at 5% and 1% respectively.

[+] and [++] indicate that the null hypotheses of statistical tests are rejected at the 5% and 1% levels of significance respectively.

[a] indicates that coefficients are multiplied by 10^1 while [b] indicates that coefficients are multiplied by 10^2.

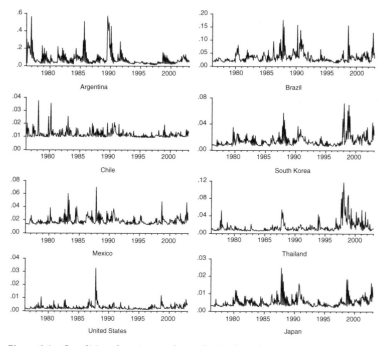

Figure 6.1 Conditional variance of sample stockmarkets

liberalization events as it was intensified when the exchange rate structure was unified into the Official Fluctuating Free Market Rate, and also when credit controls were abolished at the end of 1976. This market also becomes greatly volatile prior to its official liberalization dates in November 1989. Figure 6.2 gives a picture of monthly conditional standard deviations five years before and five years after liberalizations for sample emerging markets. As can be observed, Thailand is the only market that experienced an increase of volatility after liberalization.

Examination of standardized residuals in panel C confirms that the specified model is appropriate to fit the dynamic of monthly return series. Effectively, the estimated residuals are less correlated than the raw returns both in term of level and squared series. Only a little evidence of correlation in squared residuals at the 5 per cent level is found in Argentina. Next, the coefficients of skewness and

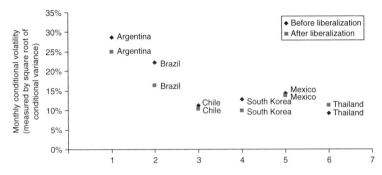

Figure 6.2 Monthly standard deviations before and after stockmarket liberalizations

excess kurtosis are, albeit significant, substantially declined. This indicates that the empirical model helps to reduce the departure from a normal distribution of monthly returns. The final and most important point to be noted here is the satisfactory feature of the bivariate GARCH(1,1) model in capturing the volatility dynamics of stock returns, as the ARCH effects disappear in the fitted residual series.

Cross-market volatility dependency

Table 6.4 presents the estimates of model coefficients, $\bar{R}^2$, block *F*-tests of VAR lags, and the Granger causality tests for estimated coefficients. A close look at the estimation results brings out that the VAR system allows us to satisfactorily explain the dependency of stockmarket volatility indices. Taking a closer look at the adjusted $\bar{R}^2$ statistics, we acknowledge that return volatility in Argentina, Brazil, South Korea, Thailand and Japan is well-explained by volatilities in other markets. For these markets, the explanatory power is generally high and ranges from 6.2 per cent (Chile) to 52.5 per cent (South Korea). The results of block *F*-tests for causality effects indicate the presence of multilateral spillover effects among sample markets. Consider for example the equation corresponding to the volatility of the Argentinean stockmarket. The results indicate that the volatility of this market is Granger-caused by the volatility in the Brazilian and Japanese stockmarkets at conventional levels, but not by other markets. We also found that the conditional volatility of the US stockmarket

Table 6.4 Causal relationships of conditional volatility across stockmarkets

Exogenous variables	Endogenous variables							
	Argentina	Brazil	Chile	South Korea	Mexico	Thailand	United States	Japan
Argentina								
β_{t-1}	0.161 (0.057)*	0.008 (0.018)	0.006 (0.003)*	0.001 (0.006)	0.009 (0.005)	0.002 (0.010)	0.002 (0.002)	0.003 (0.002)
β_{t-2}	0.588 (0.004)**	0.019 (0.014)	0.001 (0.002)	-0.003 (0.004)	-0.001 (0.004)	-0.004 (0.008)	-0.000 (0.001)	0.000 (0.001)
β_{t-3}	0.056 (0.056)	-0.015 (0.017)	-0.007 (0.003)	0.001 (0.005)	-0.006 (0.005)	-0.013 (0.010)	-0.002 (0.002)	-0.004 (0.000)*
F-statistic	70.605**	0.766	2.183^c	0.170	0.982	0.972	0.626	1.402
Brazil								
β_{t-1}	0.844 (0.275)**	0.103 (0.086)	0.022 (0.014)	0.017 (0.029)	0.064 (0.027)*	0.032 (0.051)	0.006 (0.010)	0.013 (0.009)
β_{t-2}	-0.017 (0.274)	0.164 (0.086)^c	0.008 (0.014)	0.057 (0.029)*	-0.027 (0.027)	0.000 (0.051)	-0.017 (0.010)^c	0.003 (0.009)
β_{t-3}	0.413 (0.276)	0.102 (0.086)	0.011 (0.014)	0.027 (0.029)	0.022 (0.027)*	0.015 (0.051)	0.010 (0.010)	0.015 (0.009)
F-statistic	4.459**	2.317^c	1.379	1.780	2.662*	0.186	1.571	1.805
Chile								
β_{t-1}	-0.000 (0.221)	0.151 (0.382)	0.044 (0.061)	0.079 (0.129)	0.261 (0.121)*	-0.158 (0.227)	-0.036 (0.045)	0.025 (0.043)
β_{t-2}	-0.405 (1.228)	0.338 (0.384)	0.055 (0.061)	-0.124 (0.129)	-0.161 (0.122)	-0.037 (0.228)	-0.023 (0.045)	-0.058 (0.043)
β_{t-3}	-1.082 (1.239)	0.294 (0.387)	0.047 (0.062)	-0.022 (0.131)	-0.063 (0.123)	-0.054 (0.231)	-0.003 (0.045)	0.021 (0.044)
F-statistic	0.300	0.551	0.713	0.428	2.114^c	1.100	0.324	0.782
South Korea								
β_{t-1}	-0.245 (0.687)	-0.040 (0.215)	0.009 (0.034)	0.084 (0.072)	-0.014 (0.068)	0.302 (0.127)*	-0.016 (0.025)	-0.000 (0.024)
β_{t-2}	-0.247 (0.656)	-0.393 (0.205)^c	0.016 (0.033)	0.101 (0.069)	-0.023 (0.065)	0.002 (0.122)	-0.019 (0.024)	-0.014 (0.823)
β_{t-3}	0.629 (0.661)	0.351 (207)^c	0.044 (0.033)	0.104 (0.069)	0.059 (0.065)	0.028 (0.123)	0.016 (0.024)	0.053 (0.023)*
F-statistic	0.362	2.100	0.076	2.226	0.308	1.973	0.484	1.805
Mexico								
β_{t-1}	-0.439 (0.917)	-0.182 (0.287)	-0.009 (0.046)	-0.124 (0.096)	0.056 (0.091)	-0.215 (0.170)	0.020 (0.033)	0.013 (0.032)
β_{t-2}	-0.439 (0.075)	0.272 (0.221)	0.067 (0.035)^c	0.081 (0.074)	0.582 (0.070)**	0.059 (0.130)	0.025 (0.026)	0.010 (0.025)
β_{t-3}	-1.188 (0.852)	-0.061 (0.267)	0.019(0.042)	0.050 (0.090)	-0.122 (0.084)	0.068 (0.158)	-0.033 (0.031)	-0.029 (0.030)
F-statistic	1.481	1.001	1.272	1.112	25.449**	0.713	0.756	0.431
Thailand								
β_{t-1}	0.032 (0.334)	-0.114 (0.104)	-0.006 (0.016)	0.050 (0.035)	0.038 (0.033)	0.185 (0.062)**	0.022 (0.012)^c	0.026 (0.011)*
β_{t-2}	-0.150 (0.323)	-0.070 (0.101)	-0.043 (0.016)	0.025 (0.034)	-0.006 (0.032)	0.333 (0.062)**	-0.013 (0.011)	-0.010 (0.011)

β_{t-3}	-0.095 (0.335)	-0.090 (0.105)	-0.015 (0.016)	0.114 (0.035)**	-0.035 (0.033)	0.122 (0.062)^c	-0.003 (0.012)	-0.018 (0.011)
F-statistic	0.125	0.638	0.622	7.278**	0.631	23.619**	1.350	2.110^c
United States								
β_{t-1}	-0.227 (0.656)	-0.452 (0.652)	0.023 (0.104)	-0.123 (0.220)	-0.178 (0.207)	0.453 (0.388)	0.031 (0.077)	-0.059 (0.071)
β_{t-2}	-1.171 (1.956)	0.286 (0.612)	-0.030 (0.098)	0.281 (0.206)	-0.584 (0.190)**	0.107 (0.364)	0.311 (0.069)**	0.111 (0.069)
β_{t-3}	3.727 (2.162)^c	0.545 (0.676)	0.115 (0.108)	-0.036 (0.228)	0.552 (0.214)*	-0.438 (0.402)	0.040 (0.079)	0.091 (0.074)
F-statistic	1.127	0.358	0.499	0.719	4.971**	0.638	6.650**	1.428
Japan								
β_{t-1}	-5.543 (3.474)	0.630 (1.087)	-0.239 (0.174)	0.088 (0.367)	-0.538 (0.345)	-0.054 (0.647)	0.027 (0.128)	-0.075 (0.123)
β_{t-2}	1.957 (3.001)	2.979 (0.930)**	0.067 (0.150)	1.086 (0.317)*	0.229 (0.298)	0.415 (0.559)	0.198 (0.110)^c	0.651(0.107)**
β_{t-3}	-4.444 (3.323)	-1.681 (1.039)	-0.253 (0.167)*	-0.782 (0.351)*	0.063 (0.330)	-1.035 (0.619)^c	-0.053 (0.122)	-0.224 (0.118)^c
F-statistic	2.775*	4.756**	2.556^c	6.676**	1.198	1.512	1.212	16.413**
Constant	0.066 (0.024)**	0.002 (0.007)	0.008 (0.001)**	0.002 (0.002)	0.008 (0.002)**	0.011 (0.004)**	0.001 (0.000)^c	0.001 (0.000)^c
$\bar{R}^2$	0.447	0.290	0.062	0.525	0.247	0.415	0.144	0.477

Block exogeneity test

H_0: the lags of the US volatility index do not enter in the equations for the remaining variables

Log det. Unrestricted model = -69.494 Restricted model = -69.296

$\chi^2_{(21)}$ 58.315452

(p-value = 0.00002)

H_0: the lags of the Japanese volatility index do not enter in the equations for the remaining variables

Log det. Unrestricted model = -68.422 Restricted model = -68.250

$\chi^2_{(21)}$ 50.900

(p-value = 0.00027)

Notes: $\beta_{t,i}(i = 1, 2, 3)$ is the estimated coefficient associated with volatility series in the ith market at lag $t - i$. Standard errors of estimated coefficients are in parentheses. F-statistics are empirical statistics of the Granger-causality tests applied to a block of lags of a particular variable in each equation, indicating whether variable j helps to forecast the dependent variable.

$\chi^2_{(21)}$ is the statistic of the likelihood ratio test for block exogeneity which tests whether the lags of one variable do not enter equations for the remaining variables. It has a chi-squared distribution with degrees of freedom equal to the number of restrictions. The p-values associated to likelihood ratio tests are reported in parentheses.

Log det. is the natural log of the determinant of covariance matrices of the restricted and unrestricted model.

*, ** denote statistical significance at the 5% and 1% levels respectively.

^{c} indicates statistical significance at the 10% level.

significantly causes return volatilities in only one market, Mexico. On the other hand, there is strong evidence of volatility spillovers from Japan to Argentina, Brazil and South Korea, and marginal evidence from Japan to Chile. It is worthwhile noting a regional perspective of volatility linkages. In Latin America, we recognize spillover effects from Argentina to Chile, Brazil to Argentina, Brazil to Mexico, and Chile to Mexico, while the direction of impact is from Thailand to Korea in the Asian Pacific-basin region. The geographical proximity might be, in this case, a highly accepted explanation.

One of the most intriguing questions which emerged from the above analysis is whether global markets have significant impacts on emerging-markets' volatility. For this purpose, we successively interrogate if the USA and Japan can be excluded from the VAR system. The null hypothesis considered is that the lags of the US or Japanese volatility series do not enter in the equations for the remaining variables. Since testing this null hypothesis implies cross-equation restrictions, the likelihood ratio test is then used. The results indicate that the restrictions are clearly binding because the chi-squared statistics are highly significant at the 1 per cent level (cf. Table 6.5). We henceforth conclude that lags of the US and Japan markets are not block-exogenous and play a crucial role in explaining conditional volatilities in emerging markets. The results are consistent with the findings of several asset-pricing frameworks suggesting that emerging markets exhibit some degrees of integration with world capital markets (for example Bekaert and Harvey, 1995; and Carrieri *et al.*, 2003).

Further information about the effect of foreign market volatility on each national stockmarket is also given by analysing impulse response functions (IRF). While we have computed the impulse responses from period (or month) 1 through 24, only those of three periods 1, 6 and 12 are reported in Table 6.5. Effectively, each market reacts markedly to the volatility shock in remaining markets of the system. The spillover effect leads to increased volatility for some markets and decreased volatility in others following an original shock to return volatility of a particular market. The results also indicate that the cross-market volatility responses seem to be very persistent and even last for two years after the beginning of a shock. Emerging-market volatility starts to apparently respond to volatility shock in global markets at the longer periods of time. An obvious tendency is that the impulse responses are higher between emerging markets located

Table 6.5 Impulse response function (IRFs) of sample stockmarket volatility series

Responses to shock in	Argentina	Brazil	Chile	South Korea	Mexico	Thailand	United States	Japan
Argentina								
Period 1	5.876	0.136	−0.010	0.012	0.022	−0.008	0.002	0.005
Period 6	0.773	0.015	−0.003	0.015	0.020	−0.087	−0.004	−0.002
Period 12	0.338	0.005	0.000	−0.016	0.009	−0.059	−0.002	−0.003
Brazil								
Period 1	0.000	1.833	0.054	0.239	0.339	0.113	0.108	0.152
Period 6	0.014	0.242	0.006	0.084	0.074	0.027	0.015	0.025
Period 12	−0.181	0.070	0.001	0.036	0.024	0.013	0.005	0.010
Chile								
Period 1	0.000	0.000	0.290	0.062	0.105	−0.003	0.018	0.046
Period 6	−0.311	0.063	0.008	−0.011	0.029	−0.057	−0.000	0.003
Period 12	−0.070	0.021	0.001	−0.001	0.008	−0.017	0.001	0.002
South Korea								
Period 1	0.000	0.000	0.000	0.569	0.119	0.359	0.030	0.063
Period 6	−0.625	0.000	−0.005	0.067	−0.001	0.123	0.001	0.006
Period 12	−0.303	−0.007	−0.002	0.028	0.002	0.064	0.002	0.002
Mexico								
Period 1	0.000	0.000	0.000	0.000	0.447	−0.104	0.067	0.068
Period 6	−0.867	−0.050	−0.001	−0.045	0.006	−0.072	−0.000	−0.012
Period 12	−0.343	−0.001	−0.001	−0.007	0.011	−0.018	0.001	−0.002
Thailand								
Period 1	0.000	0.000	0.000	0.000	0.000	1.022	0.022	−0.003
Period 6	−0.127	−0.063	−0.004	0.113	−0.019	0.226	0.002	0.005
Period 12	−0.180	−0.026	−0.002	0.037	−0.009	0.102	0.000	0.001
United States								
Period 1	0.000	0.000	0.000	0.000	0.000	0.000	0.170	0.027
Period 6	0.328	0.066	−0.001	−0.002	0.050	−0.003	0.008	0.002
Period 12	0.103	0.028	−0.000	0.007	0.017	−0.005	0.002	0.002
Japan								
Period 1	0.000	0.000	0.000	0.000	0.000	0.000	0.000	0.095
Period 6	−0.602	−0.095	−0.018	−0.043	0.001	−0.024	0.002	−0.016
Period 12	−0.213	−0.015	−0.004	−0.005	0.012	−0.004	0.002	−0.003

Notes: This table reports the responses (expressed in percentages) of sample markets to volatility shocks in a particular market after 1, 6 and 12 periods.

in the same region, than between emerging markets with geographical distance, and between emerging and global markets. Regarding the reactions of global markets, the results accentuate the fact that they are reasonably sensible to changes in emerging-market volatility.

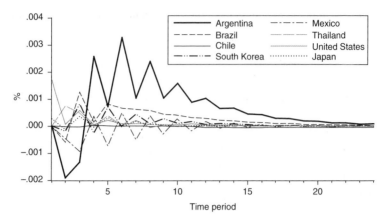

Figure 6.3   Responses of sample markets to volatility shock in the United States

To get a clear picture of these volatility transmissions, we trace the impulse responses of all markets to the volatility shock in the USA, Japan and Brazil, and results are presented in Figures 6.3 to 6.5. All other graphs are available on request. Figure 6.3 shows that the responses of sample markets to volatility shocks in the United States are generally small. For example, a one standard deviation shock to the US stockmarket of about 0.008 per cent at period 6 implies only a little reaction from foreign markets (for example −0.001 per cent in Chile, −0.002 per cent in South Korea, −0.003 per cent in Thailand, and 0.002 per cent in Japan). We note that Argentina and Mexico appear to be the most affected by the stock price changes in the US stockmarkets, by 0.328 and 0.050 per cent respectively.

Figure 6.4 depicts the impulse responses to volatility shocks issued from the Japanese market. As can be observed, emerging-market volatility responds more importantly to volatility shocks in Japan than to those in the USA. This typical spillover effect lasts about 11 periods. From period 12, the impulse responses are relatively comparable to the levels of IRF of emerging markets to the variability of the US stockmarket. In general, the volatility of most emerging markets moves together with that of Japan. At period 6 for example, a negative shock to the Japanese market generates, except for Mexico, a contemporaneous decline of volatility in all other emerging markets. Argentina also reacts remarkably to the volatility shock in Japan.

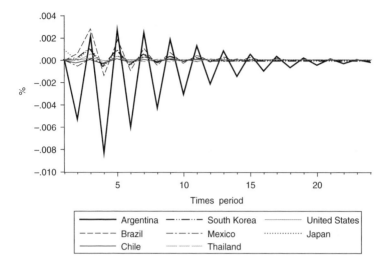

Figure 6.4 Responses of sample markets to volatility shock in Japan

Figure 6.5 depicts the volatility behaviour of foreign markets when a shock to return volatility occurred in Brazil. Surprisingly, we found that not only emerging markets, but also the US and Japanese markets have displayed substantial volatility linkages with the Brazilian market. In most cases, the spillover effect from Brazil to foreign markets is characterized by reactions in the same direction as the original shocks. An exception is the Argentinean market which moves in the opposite direction to original shocks from period 8. The interregional connection of volatility is clearly illustrated by the extensive reactions of the South Korean market volatility. Within the Latin America region, Mexico shows strong dependence on the volatility of the Brazilian market.

As noted earlier, the forecast error variance (FEV) in one market can be decomposed in parts attributable to the variation of its own shocks and shocks to conditional volatility in the remaining markets. Table 6.6 presents our results.[4] For each market, the variance decompositions add up to 100 per cent in each row. Obviously, there is a rich interaction and causality among the system volatility series. The more interesting information is found at the longer steps where the interactions between volatility series start to become considerable.

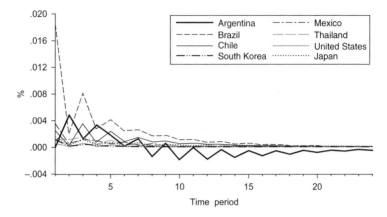

Figure 6.5 Responses of sample markets to volatility shock in Brazil

National markets explicitly exhibit some degrees of volatility dependence with foreign markets. This may be an indication that sample markets are fairly integrated among them. Below, we offer a country by country detailed discussion about the relative importance of foreign markets in the variability of stock returns in national stockmarkets:

• **Argentina**. The results from variance decompositions show that the variation of domestic volatility shocks is the main source of volatility in this market. Although the impact from foreign market volatility tends to increase with the length of the forecast horizon, it remains quite small. Mexico is the most important contributor to the volatility of Argentina with an explanatory power of about 4.60 per cent in the 12-step-ahead horizon. Among two mature markets, Japan has the greater impact on the volatility of Argentina.

• **Brazil**. The own innovations of this market count for about 99.44 and 87.98 per cent of its FEV respectively in the first step and one-year-ahead horizons. The influence of foreign market volatility on the Brazilian market is generally small, and only becomes sizable from the 2-step forecast horizon. Two years after (i.e., the 24-step forecast horizon), foreign markets contribute approximately 12.19 per cent of the global return variance in Brazil, coming mostly from Mexico with 3.84 per cent and Japan with 3.33 per cent.

- **Chile**. The FEV of the Chilean stockmarket is substantially impacted by that of Brazil, Mexico and Japan. These markets help to explain a total of about 15.17 per cent of the FEV in Chile, of which about 7.70 per cent originated from Brazil, 2.19 per cent from Mexico and 2.50 per cent from Japan. All other markets have negligible effects on return variance in the Chilean market.

- **South Korea**. It appears that the FEV of the South Korean market volatility is for the most part affected by the variance of the volatility innovations in Brazil which counts for about 14.82 per cent in the first-step forecast horizon. This indicates that the volatility transmission between the two markets is quite immediate. Besides, the effect from Brazil increases largely at the longer steps and remains stable around 34 per cent from the 9-step forecast horizon. Foreign markets including Thailand, Mexico and Japan are also responsible for the volatility of South Korea, with about 16.60 per cent of the movement of domestic market volatility due to those markets.

- **Mexico**. Nearly a half of domestic market volatility is explained by the variation of volatility innovations in foreign markets. From the 6-step ahead forecast, the most significant impacts in descending order are from Brazil, the USA, South Korea and Chile. The variance of the Japanese stockmarket volatility has a very limited effect in this case. Only at the 12-step ahead forecast does it have a contribution of 1.08 per cent to the FEV of Mexico.

- **Thailand**. Volatility innovations in South Korea and Brazil exert a significant effect on the FEV of Thailand, whereas all other foreign markets have a negligible explanatory power with respect to its return volatility. The total part of domestic market volatility explained by foreign markets stands at 26.09 percent in the 12-step forecast horizon. It is interesting to note that South Korea, as a geographical neighbour, has the strongest impacts on Thais market volatility.

- **United States**. The estimate of FEV attributable to domestic markets is, except for the first six forecast horizons, steadily close to 55 per cent. This indicates that variations of stock volatility in the US market are widely affected by volatility shock to foreign markets. We note, however, that the impact of foreign markets comes essentially from the variability of innovations in Brazilian and Mexican markets. For example, about 37.61 per cent of the domestic market variance is explained by those markets at the 12-step forecast horizon. Each of

Table 6.6 Variance decompositions of sample stockmarket volatility series

Decomposition of variance for	Standard error (×10²)	Argentina	Brazil	Chile	South Korea	Mexico	Thailand	United States	Japan
Argentina									
1-step	0.05876	100.00	0.00	0.00	0.00	0.00	0.00	0.00	0.00
6-step	0.07761	89.46	0.63	1.09	1.92	3.74	0.31	0.38	2.43
12-step	0.08144	86.80	0.74	1.11	2.68	4.60	0.31	0.53	2.87
Brazil									
1-step	0.01838	0.55	99.44	0.00	0.00	0.00	0.00	0.00	0.00
6-step	0.02216	1.42	89.24	1.55	0.17	3.39	0.50	0.63	3.06
12-step	0.02272	1.52	87.98	1.64	0.25	3.79	0.62	0.85	3.32
Chile									
1-step	0.00295	0.11	3.40	96.47	0.00	0.00	0.00	0.00	0.00
6-step	0.00314	1.75	7.29	86.15	0.41	1.72	0.40	0.02	2.22
12-step	0.00317	1.79	7.70	84.83	0.44	2.19	0.47	0.03	2.50
South Korea									
1-step	0.00621	0.03	14.82	1.01	84.11	0.00	0.00	0.00	0.00
6-step	0.00879	0.29	32.65	0.78	49.70	3.41	7.48	1.68	3.35
12-step	0.00931	0.37	34.20	0.69	46.22	4.11	8.82	1.88	3.67

Mexico									
1-step	0.00584	0.14	33.78	3.28	4.15	58.61	0.51	0.00	0.00
6-step	0.00686	1.21	31.30	3.36	3.72	54.74	0.51	4.23	0.89
12-step	0.00699	1.29	31.34	3.38	3.61	53.27	0.61	5.37	1.08
Thailand									
1-step	0.01095	0.00	1.07	0.00	10.76	0.91	87.23	0.00	0.00
6-step	0.01379	0.94	3.15	1.32	15.88	1.74	76.05	0.51	0.37
12-step	0.01460	2.07	3.15	1.39	16.78	1.72	73.91	0.47	0.46
United States									
1-step	0.00217	0.01	25.12	0.73	1.96	9.64	1.10	61.41	0.00
6-step	0.00242	0.45	25.47	0.90	2.03	11.91	2.15	56.27	0.77
12-step	0.00244	0.64	25.70	0.90	2.12	11.91	2.12	55.66	0.90
Japan									
1-step	0.00209	0.07	52.75	4.90	9.11	10.53	0.02	1.71	20.87
6-step	0.00287	0.69	54.10	3.01	7.43	10.88	1.13	4.05	18.67
12-step	0.00302	0.67	54.22	2.87	7.29	11.03	1.03	4.48	18.36

Notes: Column 2 provides the forecast error of the variable at the given forecast horizon. It results from the variation in the current and future values of the innovations to each endogenous variable in the VAR. Columns from 3 to 10 give the percentage of the forecast variance due to each innovation, with each row adding up to 100.

the remaining markets has a negligible contribution which does not exceed 3 per cent to the FEV of the USA.

• **Japan**. Except for the 1-step and 2-step horizons, the Japanese stockmarket takes only about 18 per cent of responsibility for its volatility. The remaining fraction of volatility is due to innovations in foreign markets. In particular, more than a half of its FEV is explained by the variance of volatility innovations in Brazil, Mexico, South Korea, the USA and Chile.

To summarize, global markets such as the USA and Japan do not appear, contrary to usual beliefs, to be dominant and robust to emerging markets' volatility; In all cases their impact is lower than 10 per cent. Stockmarkets of the USA, Japan, Mexico, South Korea and Thailand receive most of the volatility spillover effects from shocks to foreign market volatility. This can be potentially explained by their high degree of integration with the world financial system. It is also essential to note that Brazil is considered as the most relevant sources of volatility for sample markets, as its volatility is largely transmitted to all other markets. We are, however, unable to find a satisfactory explanation behind the dominant role of the Brazilian market volatility.

Liberalizations, volatility and spillover effects

In examining emerging-market volatility, two questions are of strong interest for market participants: Do stock market openings strengthen emerging-market volatility? And is the international transmission of volatility between emerging and global markets increased after market openings?

Here, we apply the simplest approach commonly used in empirical literature to examine the first issue. It consists of regressing the fitted stockmarket volatility series on four dummy variables of market liberalization. BEFORE refers to 36 months prior to the official dates of market openings; PRE is 30 months to six months prior to official dates of liberalization; DURING corresponds to six months prior to three months after official liberalizations; POST is four months after official liberalizations to the end of the estimation period. The dates of market openings for selected emerging markets are official dates provided by Bekaert and Harvey (2000). Table 6.7 reports our results.

Table 6.7 Stockmarket liberalizations and conditional volatility

		Financial liberalization indicators				
	CONST	BEFORE	PRE	DURING	POST	$\bar{R}^2$
Argentina	0.091**	0.096	-0.127	0.158**	-0.039**	0.297
	(0.011)	(0.095)	(0.096)	(0.036)	(0.012)	
Brazil	0.033**	0.028**	-0.011	0.010*	-0.002	0.093
	(0.002)	(0.006)	(0.009)	(0.004)	(0.003)	
Chile	0.012**	-0.000	0.001	0.001*	-0.001**	0.047
	(0.000)	(0.000)	(0.001)	(0.000)	(0.000)	
South Korea	0.013**	0.002**	0.001	-0.001	0.002	0.013
	(0.000)	(0.000)	(0.002)	(0.000)	(0.001)	
Mexico	0.018**	-0.001	0.006^c	0.001	0.000	0.032
	(0.000)	(0.003)	(0.003)	(0.003)	(0.001)	
Thailand	0.009**	-0.021**	0.021**	0.021**	0.009**	0.103
	(0.000)	(0.002)	(0.002)	(0.002)	(0.002)	
All markets	0.029	0.017	-0.017	0.032	-0.004	0.034
	(0.002)	(0.050)	(0.050)	(0.031)	(0.003)	

Notes: *, ** denote statistical significance at the 5% and 1% levels respectively. ^{c} indicates statistical significance at the 10% level.

Globally, the findings suggest a strong relationship between stock-market liberalization and market volatility. First, it is observed that conditional volatility significantly increases in Brazil and South Korea by 2.8 and 0.2 per cent per month respectively before liberalizations, while it decreases by 2.1 per cent per month in Thailand. Second, the pre-liberalization period is characterized by the rising of volatility in two markets, Thailand and Mexico. Next, the evidence from DURING coefficients indicates that volatility is raised in four markets including Argentina, Brazil, Chile and Thailand. Finally, the results for the post-liberalization period are mixed according to the POST coefficients. We recognize a monthly increase of about 0.9 per cent in the Thai market volatility. Specifically, market openings significantly lead to a monthly diminution of 3.9 per cent and 0.1 per cent in the volatility of Argentina and Chile. In three remaining markets, stock volatility neither increases nor decreases in the aftermath of liberalizations. The conflicting findings are, in our opinion, due to country-specific liberalization strategies and market microstructure. The results from cross-market regression analysis provide evidence that,

Table 6.8 Comparison of volatility dependencies before and after financial liberalizations: March 1976–Sept. 1989 versus Oct. 1989–Jan. 2003

Endogenous variables	Exogenous variables								$\bar{R}^2$
	Argentina	Brazil	Chile	South Korea	Mexico	Thailand	United States	Japan	
Argentina									
F-statistic (B)	16.754**	4.451**	0.785	1.311	1.764	0.351	1.258	0.636	0.356
F-statistic (A)	67.479**	1.845	2.492^c	0.868	1.078	0.420	1.054	1.101	0.668
Brazil									
F-statistic (B)	0.368	1.484	0.191	1.388	1.163	1.539	1.574	3.999**	0.335
F-statistic (A)	2.802*	0.866	2.991*	0.205	0.769	0.595	0.691	0.724	0.260
Chile									
F-statistic (B)	1.995	1.629	0.128	0.759	1.622	1.836	0.423	0.722	0.016
F-statistic (A)	2.241^c	10.276**	2.533^c	0.204	5.903**	1.846	1.810	2.722*	0.433
South Korea									
F-statistic (B)	0.770	0.653	0.564	2.594^c	1.089	0.451	1.819	5.614**	0.591
F-statistic (A)	0.091	2.229^c	0.946	0.329	2.429^c	6.084**	1.473	2.340^c	0.501
Mexico									
F-statistic (B)	1.435	4.387**	3.047*	0.553	18.574**	2.174^c	3.626*	1.191	0.306
F-statistic (A)	1.227	1.515	0.797	0.222	1.166	0.405	2.280^c	0.243	0.208
Thailand									
F-statistic (B)	0.250	1.834	0.812	0.949	0.118	5.718**	0.584	1.470	0.288
F-statistic (A)	0.413	0.158	0.855	1.421	0.775	6.796**	1.071	1.264	0.366
United States									
F-statistic (B)	0.564	2.729*	0.297	0.686	0.641	3.669*	2.120	1.257	0.155
F-statistic (A)	0.591	0.353	0.336	0.145	0.486	1.901^c	2.544	0.892	0.197
Japan									
F-statistic (B)	1.862	3.696*	0.825	0.180	0.970	2.957*	0.968	10.301**	0.477
F-statistic (A)	1.148	1.852	0.975	0.607	0.572	1.152	2.019	4.395**	0.495

Notes: B: before liberalizations. A: after liberalizations. See also notes to Table 6.4 for the significance of the *F*-statistic.
*, ** denote statistical significance at the 5% and 1% levels respectively. ^{c} indicates statistical significance at the 10% level.

on average, emerging-market volatility remains unaffected following stockmarket liberalizations.

To reach an answer to the second question, the VAR model is reestimated over the pre- and post-liberalization periods. Since most of sample stockmarkets were liberalized at the end of the 1980s, the pre-liberalization period is chosen to be the sub-period from March 1976 to September 1989, while the post-liberalization period refer to October 1989 to January 2003. Table 6.8 reports the block *F*-tests and adjusted $\bar{R}^2$ statistics for pre- versus post-liberalization samples. The results indicate that return volatility is largely transmitted among markets in both sample periods. Compared to the pre-liberalization period, there is ample evidence of increased volatility transmission after liberalizations in three emerging markets – Argentina, Chile and Thailand – and both mature markets. In other emerging markets, the explanatory power of the corresponding equations is slightly reduced.

Concluding remarks

In summary, the objective of this chapter has been to examine the level of volatility in six emerging stockmarkets and volatility dependencies between these markets and two global markets, the USA and Japan. We have also tried to relate both issues to stockmarket liberalizations which have been embarked on in emerging countries over the last two decades. The rationale is that empirical results of such studies may allow investors to determine the appropriate asset-pricing rules in emerging markets, and thus to make optimal portfolio allocations. On the other hand, policy-makers can learn more about the effects of their political changes on stockmarkets, and therefore adopt additional measures to insure financial stability if necessary. The most interesting results are the following.

First, our empirical findings indicate that emerging-market volatility is substantially affected by stockmarket volatility in the USA and Japan as shown by the Granger-causality test and the likelihood ratio test for block exogeneity. This may be suggestive to the view that the financial liberalization process helps to further integrate emerging markets into the global financial system. Unfortunately, this hypothesis appears to be unverified based on our pre- and post-liberalization analysis because there is no obvious tendency of increasing international linkages between emerging and mature markets in the aftermath of financial liberalizations.

Second, the results from impulse-response analysis are very intriguing, in the sense that emerging-markets' volatility tends to react more importantly to the structural shocks from other emerging markets, especially emerging markets of the same region, than to the structural shocks that originated in the two developed markets. As a result, we think that geographical proximity and market nature similarities are of paramount importance for volatility spillovers.

Finally, over the six emerging markets examined in this study, we found that market openings significantly led to less volatile markets in two cases, and contributed to an increase of stockmarket volatility in only one case. For the remaining emerging markets, it is shown that the variability of stockmarket returns was not impacted by the actual financial liberalizations. These country-specific evidences concerning the effect of financial liberalization can be reasonably explained, if not certainly for the most part, by the differences in the liberalization tactics which have been used to liberalize emerging markets, and also by the differences in the domestic market infrastructures. In addition, our bivariate GARCH-M model for stockmarket volatility, whose goal is to incorporate the influence of global markets on domestic market volatility, can be applied to other emerging markets in order to obtain a categorical answer regarding how market deregulations impact stockmarket volatility.

Notes

1. As recently as March 2002, S&P's emerging market databases have covered 34 emerging markets and 20 frontier markets which are one step from obtaining emerging-market status, compared to only 24 emerging markets covered in 1985. During the same period, the importance of emerging markets to the world has rapidly increased as well: by 1982 the ratio of emerging markets' capitalization to world market capitalization was only 2.5%, while it stood at 8.5% by the end of 1999 (see S&P's *Emerging Stock Markets Factbook*, 2000, p. 19). Specifically, electronic trading systems are installed in many emerging-market countries.

2. The trade-off of using this procedure is between understated standard errors due to unknown sampling errors in the first estimation step, and the large number of markets which can be handled in the study. In fact, a multivariate GARCH is preferred in order to avoid this disadvantage, but the

risk is that the estimation of the model is computationally difficult because of the proliferation of parameters to be estimated.
3. The insignificant relationships between returns and volatility in international equity markets have been documented in several studies (see for example Baillie and DeGennaro, 1990, for empirical evidence in US stockmarkets, and Mougoue and Whyte, 1996, for empirical evidence in German and French equity markets).
4. The whole table of FEV decompositions is available on request to the author.

References

Aggarwal, R., Inclan, C. and Leal, R. (1999) 'Volatility in Emerging Stock Markets', *Journal of Financial and Quantitative Analysis*, vol. 34, pp. 33–55.

Baillie, R. and DeGennaro, R.P. (1990) 'Stock Returns and Volatility', *Journal of Financial and Quantitative Analysis*, vol. 25, pp. 203–14.

Bekaert, G. and Harvey, C.R. (1995) 'Time-Varying World Market Integration', *Journal of Finance*, vol. 50, pp. 403–44.

Bekaert, G. and Harvey, C.R. (1997) 'Emerging Equity Market Volatility', *Journal of Financial Economics*, vol. 43, pp. 29–78.

Bekaert, G. and Harvey, C.R. (2000) 'Foreign Speculators and Emerging Equity Markets', *Journal of Finance*, vol. 55, pp. 565–613.

Bekaert, G. and Harvey, C.R. (2003) 'Emerging Markets Finance', *Journal of Empirical Finance*, vol. 10, pp. 3–55.

Bekaert, G., Harvey, C.R. and Lundblad, C. (2001) 'Emerging Equity Markets and Economic Growth', *Journal of Development Economics*, vol. 66, pp. 465–504.

Bollerslev, T. (1986) 'Generalized Autoregressive Conditional Heteroscedasticity', *Journal of Econometrics*, vol. 31, pp. 307–27.

Bollerslev, T. (1990) 'Modelling the Coherence in Short-run Nominal Exchange Rates: A Multivariate Generalized ARCH Model', *Review of Economics and Statistics*, vol. 72, pp. 498–505.

Bollerslev, T. and Wooldridge, J. (1992) 'Quasi-Maximum Likelihood Estimations and Inferences in Dynamic Models with Time-Varying Covariances', *Econometric Reviews*, vol. 11, pp. 143–72.

Bollerslev, T., Engle, R.F. and Wooldridge, J. (1988) 'A Capital Asset Pricing Model with Time-Varying Covariances', *Journal of Political Economy*, vol. 96, pp. 116–31.

Carrieri, F., Errunza, V. and Hogan, K. (2003) 'Characterizing World Market Integration through Time', *McGill University Working Paper*.

Claessens, S., Dasgupta, S. and Glen, J. (1995) 'Return Behaviour in Emerging Stock Markets', *World Bank Economic Review*, vol. 9, pp. 131–51.

DeSantis, G. and Imrohoroglu, S. (1997) 'Stock Returns and Volatility in Emerging Financial Markets', *Journal of International Money and Finance*, vol. 16, pp. 561–79.

Enders, W. (1995) *Applied Econometric Time Series*, Wiley Series in Probability and Mathematical Statistics (New York: John Wiley & Sons, Inc.).

Engle, R.F. (1982) 'Autoregressive Conditional Heteroscedasticity with Estimates of the Variance of UK Inflation', *Econometrica*, vol. 50, pp. 987–1008.

Engle, R.F. and Kroner, K.F. (1993) 'Multivariate Simultaneous Generalized ARCH', Working Paper, University of California, San Diego.

Engle, R.F., Chou, R.Y. and Kroner, K.F. (1992) 'ARCH Modelling in Finance', *Journal of Econometrics*, vol. 52, pp. 5–59.

Hamao, Y., Masulis, R.W. and Ng, V. (1990) 'Correlations in Changes and Volatility Across International Stock Markets', *Review of Financial Studies*, vol. 3, pp. 281–307.

Harvey, C.R. (1995) 'Predictable Risk and Returns in Emerging Markets', *Review of Financial Studies*, vol. 8, pp. 773–816.

He, L.T. (2001) 'Time Variation Paths of International Transmission of Stock Volatility – US vs. Hong Kong and South Korea', *Global Finance Journal*, vol. 12, pp. 79–93.

Karolyi, G.A. (1995) 'A Multivariate GARCH Model of International Transmission of Stock Returns and Volatility: The Case of the United States and Canada', *Journal of Business and Economic Statistics*, vol. 13, pp. 11–25.

Kearney, C. (2000) 'The Determination and International Transmission of Stock Market Volatility', *Global Finance Journal*, vol. 11, pp. 31–52.

Kim, E.H. and Singal, V. (2000) 'Stock Market Openings: Experience of Emerging Economies', *Journal of Business*, vol. 73, pp. 25–66.

Leachman, L. and Francis, B. (1996) 'Equity Market Return Volatility: Dynamics and Transmission among the G-7 Countries', *Global Finance Journal*, vol. 7, pp. 27–52.

Levich, R.M. (2001) 'The Importance of Emerging Capital Markets', Working Paper, New York University.

Liu, Y.A. and Pan, M.S. (1997) 'Mean and Volatility Spillover Effects in the US and Pacific-Basin Stock Markets', *Multinational Finance Journal*, vol. 1, pp. 47–62.

Miles, W. (2002) 'Financial Deregulation and Volatility in Emerging Equity Markets', *Journal of Economic Development*, vol. 27, pp. 113–26.

Mougoué, M. and Whyte, A.M. (1996) 'Stock Returns and Volatility: An empirical Investigation of the German and French Equity Markets', *Global Finance Journal*, vol. 7, pp. 253–63.

Schwert, G.M. (1989) 'Why Does Stock Volatility Change Over Time', *Journal of Finance*, vol. 44, pp. 1115–53.

Standard & Poor's, *Emerging Stock Markets Factbook 2000* (New York, Standard & Poor's).

7
The Baghdad Stock Exchange: A Dismal First Decade ... A Growth Path Ahead?

Kadom J.A. Shubber and Talal A. Kadhim

Introduction

The formal re-start of the Baghdad Stock Exchange in late June 2004 can be viewed as a stepping stone in the arduous process of socioeconomic reconstruction of this ancient land, whose people have suffered so painfully over the past three decades in particular. Owing to the enormous resources – both apparent and potential – which Iraq happens to possess, a healthy market for financial assets can greatly assist in enabling the country to stand on its feet, helping thereby in oiling the positive cycle of economic regeneration and general development of the country.

Some may, however, contend that it is ironic to speak of a potential thriving market for financial securities within the current turbulent climate in Iraq. Yet, judging by the experiences of other emerging economies in Africa, Asia and Eastern Europe, where totalitarian regimes were swept aside – and considering the particular circumstances of Iraq – it had always been expected that a period of chaos would ensue after Saddam's fall from power.

What is vitally significant in this regard is that those in positions of authority have a critical stake in accomplishing stability and enabling the country to stand back on its feet. It is clearly in the interests of the United States and Britain, as well as most Iraqi politicians, that a viable system is built afresh, encompassing the national economy, a generally-acceptable constitution, a solid industrial base, rehabilitated social fabric, an independent judiciary, and functioning political institutions.

The 1990s saw dramatic growth in the number of stock exchanges around the world. At the start of the decade, the World Federation of Exchanges (WFE) had 38 members.[1] In mid-2004, the Federation had 54 members, while additional small regional federations include dozens of other exchanges – in places such as Oman, Kazakhstan and Romania – which had not qualified for WFE membership.[2]

Once stability is attained, Iraq's economy has the capacity to accomplish steady growth. Remarkable progress can be achieved by several major sectors, prominent among which are those connected with oil and gas, encompassing crude oil production, natural gas, oil refining and petrochemicals. Other important sectors of the Iraqi economy include minerals, construction materials, agriculture, chemicals, textiles/ clothing, building and food/beverages.

The development of these sectors will require enormous funding, particularly in view of wide-ranging devastation brought about by wars, internal strife and terrorist activity. It has even been suggested that firms involved in oil production and other sub-sectors of the hydrocarbon sector could at least be partly privatized, in order to facilitate financing, growth and professional management.

As Iraq's economy is likely to be dominated in the future by the private sector, an efficient stockmarket can open the gates for the setting up of scores of new enterprises, as well as the expansion and development of existing businesses. The adoption of a liberal economic policy would be highly beneficial, so as to permit investment from outside, including Iraqis living aboard, nationals of Gulf countries and investors based in Arab, Muslim and other regions.

An additional and relevant factor is the strong possibility for some form of regional economic grouping, whereby Iraq may join neighbours in the context of a regional bloc. Iraq's partners in such a grouping may be fellow Arab nations (for example Jordan, Kuwait, Syria) or adjacent Muslim countries (such as Turkey, Iran). Cooperation of this sort would allow heightened cross-border trade and investment.

Background

The Baghdad Stock Exchange was formally set up for the first time in 1992, two years after the imposition of stringent economic sanctions by the international community. These penalties were the

most severe meted out by the United Nations since its establishment in the aftermath of the Second World War, and were put
together in the wake of Saddam's reckless invasion of Kuwait in
summer 1990.

Arguably, the establishment of the Stock Exchange was an attempt
by the regime to give the appearance of normality to the national
economy, and that it was in a healthy shape, despite the impact of
economic sanctions. The majority of companies which came to be
quoted on the Exchange were ex-public-sector enterprises which
were privatized during the 1980s, when the government launched
what was labelled as a policy of 'economic restructuring'. Under the
pretext of ridding the public sector of 'poorly-performing' or 'high-
cost' establishments, many enterprises were sold off, and for the most
part the new owners were people/families having close links to the
ruling clique.

A prominent Iraqi economist, Dr Muhammad Ali Zainy (2003),
wrote in this regard:[3]

> The stock market in Iraq was feeble and extremely limited in
> scope, and the number of investors very small. The government of
> the day did not make any serious effort to attract small investors
> among ordinary people, so as to take part in purchasing the assets
> that were about to be sold off, resulting in effect to the confinement
> of the new owners within a limited group.

Zainy (2003) goes on to point out that out of 70 manufacturing
establishments that were privatized, one family was able to have a
controlling stake in 13 of those companies.[4] He adds that the majority of privatized industrial and agricultural companies found their
way to 'peripheral groups' who had no worthwhile links to Iraqi
industry, commerce and agriculture, while the prime feature of
the new owners was probably their attachment to top officials in the
regime, being adjuncts to those in authority and amongst their
staunchest supporters.[5]

There is strong evidence to indicate that the privatization programme
involved selling the assets at rock bottom prices, as the government
only asked for a downpayment of 40 per cent, while the remainder
could be settled through instalments.[6] Chaundry (1991) elaborates
on this by noting that privatization efforts in Iraq during that period
did not attain the objectives set out, such as increased output and

augmenting reserves of foreign exchange, but instead spawned higher rates of inflation, widespread unemployment, paucity of basic goods, widened gaps in income distribution, and the spread of a parallel (black) market in foreign currencies.[7]

It must be said that the overall value of quoted shares at the time painted a pathetic profile of the exchange, and did not do justice to a major oil-producing country rich with natural resources, and having an industrial base that was relatively developed by regional standards. The overall market capitalization of quoted firms in early 2003 hardly corresponded to the value of the country's weekly crude oil exports at the time.

In early 2003, 115 companies were quoted on the Baghdad Stock Exchange, most of which were partly State-owned.[8] The estimated market capitalization of all 115 companies quoted did not exceed ID 600 billion, corresponding to $400 million at the time. Official guidelines did not permit share prices to move in excess of 5 per cent in any one session.[9] At the time, the Exchange was holding one three-hour session three days each week, while most of those attending did not give the impression of being serious investors.[10] In fact, evidence indicated strongly that those present were mostly retired people who viewed the session as a social venue to meet friends and exchange thoughts, rather than to consider down-to-earth investment decisions.

It was reported that prices on the Baghdad Exchange were up by 37 per cent in the first few months of 2003, as investors were buying 'aggressively ahead of the anticipated ousting of the regime'.[11] Much of the stock subsequently became worthless, as many of the then listed companies had relied on their ties to the defunct regime, and consequently became bankrupt.

Table 7.1 presents some relevant figures concerning four other exchanges in the region, for the years 1999–2003. All the four bourses relate to countries that are much smaller that Iraq in terms of population, wealth, economic development and potential for development.

Strengths and weaknesses

Once stability and security are attained, Iraqis can expect to see a relatively high rate of sustainable development, due to the country's enormous wealth of natural resources. The latter include much fertile

Table 7.1 Prime indicators for four Middle Eastern stockmarkets (1999–2003)

Stockmarket and indicators	1999	2000	2001	2002	2003
Amman Stock Exchange					
(i) No. of firms quoted	152	163	161	158	161
(ii) Market capitalization (JD m.)	4,138	3,510	4,477	5,029	7,773
(iii) Market capitalization (US$ m.)	5,836	4,950	6,314	7,092	10,962
Beirut Stock Exchange					
(i) No. of firms quoted	13	13	14	13	14
(ii) Market capitalization (US$ m.)	1,921	1,583	1,248	1,395	1,503
Dubai Stock Exchange					
(i) No. of firms quoted	n.a.	12	13	14	16
(ii) Market capitalization (AE Dirham m.)	n.a.	21,564	30,539	36,447	55,465
(iii) Market capitalization (US$ m.)	–	5,870	8,314	9,923	15,100
Bahrain Stock Exchange					
(i) No. of firms quoted	n.a.	n.a.	n.a.	40	41
(ii) Market capitalization (BD m.)	n.a.	n.a.	n.a.	4,459	5,806
(iii) Market capitalization (US$ m.)	–	–	–	1,681	2,189

Sources and notes:
- For Amman's bourse: www.ammanstockex.com (6 October 2004). The JD/US$ currency exchange rate was taken on 19 Dec. 2004 from www.Forex-Markets.com (rate $1 = JD 0.7091).
- For the Beirut Stock Exchange: www.bse.com (6 October 2004). US dollar values for market capitalization were given on this website.
- Figures on Dubai are taken from: www.dfm.co.ae (11 October 2004). The exchange rate was taken from the *Financial Times*, 17 Dec. 2004 ($1 = AE D 3.673).
- Figures relating to Bahrain were obtained from: www.bahrainstock.com. The US$ exchange rate was taken from the *Financial Times*, 17 Dec. 2004 (US$ = 0.377 BD).

land, reasonable availability of water, a variety of mineral resources, in addition to the pivotal role of huge oil reserves.

Table 7.2 gives the size of Iraq's population, GDP figures and per capital GDP for five selected years over the period 1980–2000. GDP figures (as well as per capital GDP) in this table are in constant 1980 prices, and assume a US dollar/Iraqi dinar exchange of $3.3 to the dinar, a rate which at the time was a fair reflection of the Iraqi currency's value.

Another major factor is the relatively well-developed profile of human resources, when Iraq is compared with neighbouring nations. This is reflected in the proportion of the adult population who have

Table 7.2 Iraqi gross domestic product and per capital
GDP, selected years 1980–2000 (constant 1980 prices)

Year	Population (million)	GDP (ID m.)	Per capita GDP (ID)
1980	13.3	15,648	1,177
1985	15.6	10,921	700
1990	18.1	13,863	766
1995	20.0	2,961	148
2000	22.9	7,417	324

Source: Zainy (2003), p. 322.

gained a degree/qualification from higher/further education institutions, or otherwise have acquired a practical skill.

In addition, there is much accumulated industrial experience in the country when we consider all types of establishments within the economy, whether in the private, public, mixed or cooperative sectors. The seeds of modern industrial development were sown during the 1930s, 1940s, and 1950s when new enterprises were set up, some of which were joint-stock companies.

During that epoch, dealing in the shares of those firms was made possible through social contacts, and often facilitated by the management of respective firms. Over that period, a few major plants (for example cement-making projects) were founded by the government, with the intention of selling them to the public when they became well-established and commercially viable.[12] A number of nationally-owned industrial projects in the private sector

were set up during this period, but these were viewed as insufficient for tapping the country's potential and meeting the growth rates which had been hoped for. Consequently, foreign enterprises were provided with certain incentives to invest in the country, particularly when such investment was directed towards the establishments of relatively large or medium-sized types of industrial projects.[13]

In today's climate, an efficient and expanding bourse for financial securities can attract sizeable investment funds from several quarters, not least of which are the Iraqi expatriate community and investors based in neighbouring Arab and Muslim countries. On the assumption that Iraq will be allowing foreign incoming investment, many Western and Japanese investors may consider Iraqi firms for inclusion in their portfolios of financial assets, particularly in the case of investing institutions such as pension funds, banks, investment firms and insurance companies.

It must, however, be recognized that certain weaknesses do persist in this regard, and these require urgent attention. In particular, the legal, regulatory and administrative frameworks for an efficient, fair and transparent financial market need to be put together.

Writing in the *Christian Science Monitor*, Teicher (2004) points out that

> as Romanians and Mongolians and others are finding out, sometimes the hard way, what matters most is the infrastructure – the set of rules and enforcement mechanisms that govern the process. And getting that right balance can be tricky in places not in tune with free enterprise.[14]

In Iraq, the challenge is to replace an erstwhile corrupt system with something far more open, fair and practical. Technology is another issue for the nascent Iraqi market. Previously, each listed firm 'kept its own records, so the new exchange needs an electronic depository to track prices, trades, and shareholder identity numbers'.[15]

On re-opening in June 2004, no electronic system was employed. Each market intermediary took a stand adjacent to a large board bearing company share prices, to record changes and new information pertinent to each stock. However, the market's management board have declared their intention to incorporate an electronic trading system.[16]

Clearly, therefore, it is of paramount importance that newly-established frameworks ensure the availability of timely and accurate corporate information, so that investors may be able to take rational and well-considered decisions. Proper procedures must be laid out for initial public offerings, announcements of new information, declarations of financial results, default on financial commitments and issues of additional financial assets by quoted firms. An overhaul of the whole administrative set-up of the exchange is needed, and the institution ought to be privately run with some oversight by public bodies, including the Central Bank, Financial Control Organization and the Ministry of Finance.

Prospects

On its resumption of trading in June 2004, the Baghdad Stock Exchange had 27 firms listed, with a total number of 74 billion shares.[17] This event came after several attempts to get a re-start, and at the time trading was taking place inside a hotel lounge area.

Reports from Baghdad indicated increasing interest from other firms, and the market's management expected the number of firms quoted to rise gradually. The market was opening for two days each week, and the average number of shares traded was around 500 million, with a total value of some ID 3 billion.[18]

A source at a regional investment bank expressed the view that the Baghdad market would offer regional and international investors 'an opportunity to test Iraq's financial waters without over-committing in a high risk country'.[19] In January 2004, the said source (Jordan-based Atlas Investment Group) published a comprehensive guide to Iraq's capital market, containing research on 115 companies which were set to re-list, as well as more than 40 formerly State-owned enterprises that were likely to become quoted on the market.[20]

For several months prior to the final re-start of the Baghdad bourse, Atlas Investment was involved in efforts to identify locally-based brokers and to bring them together with officials who were in charge of restarting the bourse.[21] A director of Atlas, Omar Masri, had visited New York, where he met institutional clients investing in Jordanian and Palestinian companies. Masri encouraged them to 'consider the nascent Iraqi market for undervalued opportunities that offer long-term growth'.[22]

Moreover, Masri teamed up with New York's Auerbach Grayson and Co. Inc., which is a boutique brokerage steering US institutions towards foreign investments, via a world-wide network of partner firms.[23] Since summer 2003, Auerbach Grayson was urging to get the Baghdad Stock Exchange running, and its executives expressed some frustration at the lack of urgency shown by the US administration in Baghdad at the time.

Clearly, efforts had been dented by the continuing violence in the city, and by the former emphasis on courting foreign direct investment rather than investment in financial assets. Some would argue that the failure to re-start the Baghdad exchange at an earlier point was indicative of the broader setbacks in reconstructing the Iraqi economy. Undoubtedly, the coming months will not be easy, in terms of the general security situation, as well as efforts to rebuild the national economy and institutions of civil society.

All in all, if we take a positive stance and assume that Iraq will become stable politically and prosperous economically, then the opportunities for the country's bourse are enormous. On a 10-year horizon, the number of quoted firms could multiply several times over, and the total market capitalization of all firms listed could exceed previous figures by a substantial margin.

It is noteworthy that in the late 1970s and early 1980s, Iraq had a large number of industrial firms in a variety of industrial sectors. Official figures show that in 1977 there existed a total of 43,267 industrial firms of various sizes (oil extraction exempted), both in terms of the number of employees and value of output.[24] Unfortunately, no corresponding recent figures are available, but it is fair to expect that a degree of growth has been achieved in this regard.

The 1977 figure quoted above included 1,548 large and medium-sized firms (outside oil extraction), representing just under 4 per cent of the total.[25] At the time, those large and medium-sized firms employed over 150,000 people and had a combined output of about $2,400 m.[26] If we extrapolate these figures, it is probably reasonable to hypothesize that thousands of medium and large firms presently exist in Iraq in various sectors of the economy.

Conclusions

While the present state of the political, economic and social affairs of the country provides only a limited scope for optimism, this chapter has focused essentially on the medium and long-term perspective. As most of those wielding effective power and influence would benefit greatly from a stable and prosperous Iraq, the argument presented here suggests that the country should be back on its feet when key sectors (oil, financial services, construction, government organs, trade, transport and so on) become normalized in due course. This would set the stage for economic activity to flow in an orderly fashion, and for business investment and economic development to take off. Once this is attained, the resumption of the growth and prosperity of the Stock Exchange can be expected in a serious way, though it is necessary to embark first on a programme to reform the administrative structure and ensure a new legal and regulatory framework for the proper functioning of the institution.

Available information indicates that officials in Baghdad are preparing for a massive privatization of State-owned companies, though the process is not expected to be finalized until an elected government is in place next year (2005).[27] Authorities in Baghdad have published new commercial laws, and have been reforming Iraq's accounting practices to meet Western standards.[28]

This chapter contends that once the country achieves stability in terms of its political and economic system, a thriving bourse for financial securities can play a prime role in attracting investor interest, provision of finance for corporate growth and development, and the setting-up of scores of new businesses in a variety of economic sectors. A reformed, efficient and transparent stock exchange can be a catalyst for procuring much-needed funds for industrial development, providing in the process the vital ingredient of confidence in the functioning of the whole economic-cum-political system.

Stock exchanges can play a pivotal role in the economies of developing nations. They help firms to procure capital from domestic and foreign sources, and create opportunities to smaller investors who are keen for a chance to convert their stocks into cash. By showing which companies' or sectors' stock prices are rising relative to others, bourses signal where new money should be invested.

Moreover, as Iraqis move forward, they can benefit from the experiences of countries that have recently been transforming their economies from the State-owned model. In Russia and several other former Eastern-bloc countries, there have been some large-scale privatization schemes intended to construct free-market economies and modern stockmarket operations. These experiences have been mixed in terms of their success, as many former public-sector firms were ill-prepared for the private sector. For instance, many investors lost money due to fraud and/or the undeveloped nature of the legal-cum-regulatory infrastructure.

We therefore need to be mindful that this may take place in Iraq's case. Both the number of any such instances and their seriousness, as well as the potential growth and role of the nascent exchange, will necessarily be a function of the maturity of the legal-cum-regulatory infrastructures, in addition to the competence of the bourse's management.

Notes

1. A. Teicher (2004), 'Coming Soon: Stock Trades in Baghdad', *The Christian Science Monitor*, 2 February.
2. *Ibid*.
3. M.A. Zainy (2003), 'The Iraqi Economy: Past, Present and Future Alternatives', Al-Rafid Ltd, p. 197. This publication is in Arabic.
4. *Ibid*.
5. *Ibid*.
6. K.A. Chaundry (1991), 'On the Way to Market, Economic Liberalization and Iraq's Invasion of Kuwait', in *Middle East Report*, May–June 1991, p. 18; cited in M.A. Zainy, *ibid*., p. 197.
7. K.A. Chaundry, *ibid*., p. 18.
8. R. Khalaf (2003), 'Business as Usual: Baghdad's Bourse Ignores Threats of War', *Financial Times*, London, 22 February, p. 22.
9. *Ibid*.
10. *Ibid*.
11. S. McCarthy (2004), 'Few Listings, but Iraq Index May Rise from Rubble', globe and mail.com, 7 May 2004, p. B1.
12. K.J.A. Shubber (1985), 'An Assessment of the Determinants of Packaging in Technology Transfers to Developing Countries: A Theoretical and Empirical Study', unpublished doctoral thesis, Loughborough University of Technology, April 1985, p. 218.
13. *Ibid*.
14. A. Teicher, *op. cit.*
15. *Ibid*.
16. *Al-Khaleej* newspaper. Quoted from www.alkhaleej.ae/articles (27 July 2004).
17. www.menafn.com (27 July 2004). Middle East North Africa Financial Network.
18. *Ibid*.
19. Ft.com. London cited in Proquest.Umi.com (Proquest document ID 528343971).
20. *Ibid*.
21. McCarthy, *op. cit.*, p. B1.
22. *Ibid*.
23. *Ibid*.
24. K.J.A. Shubber, *op. cit.*, p. 231.
25. *Ibid*.
26. *Ibid*.
27. S. McCarthy, *op. cit.*
28. *Ibid*.

References

Al-Khaleej newspaper (27 July 2004), quoted from www.alkhaleej.ae/articles

Chaundry, K.A. (1991) 'On the Way to Market, Economic Liberalization and Iraq's Invasion of Kuwait', *Middle East Report*, May–June 1991, cited in M.A. Zainy (2003) *The Iraqi Economy: Past, Present and Future Options*, Al-Rafid Ltd.

FT.com. London, cited in Proquest, Umi.com (Proquest document ID 528343971).

Khalaf, R. (2003) 'Business as Usual: Baghdad's Bourse Ignores Threats of War', *Financial Times*, London, 22 February.

McCarthy, S. (2004) 'Few Listings, but Iraq Index May Rise from Rubble', Globe and mail.com, 7 May.

Shubber, K.J.A. (1985) 'An Assessment of the Determinants of Packaging in Technology Transfers to Developing Countries: A Theoretical and Empirical Study', unpublished doctoral thesis, Loughborough University of Technology, April 1985. *Times*, London, 22 February 2003.

Teicher, A. (2004) 'Coming Soon: Stock Trades in Baghdad', *The Christian Science Monitor*, 2 February.

Zainy, M.A. (2003) *The Iraqi Economy: Past, Present and Future Options*, Al-Rafid Ltd. This publication is in Arabic.

www.ammanstockex.com (6 October 2004).

www.bse.com

www.bahrainstock.com

www.dfm.co.ae

www.menafn.com (27 July 2004). Middle East North Africa Financial Network.

8

Risk Management and Securitization of Assets: The Case of Iraq

Ola Sholarin

Introduction

Well before the second Gulf War started in March 2003, many analysts wrote about the economics of the war. In their arguments, they contended that billions of dollars would be needed to fight the war. Twelve months after the war has officially 'ended', economic planners and analysts are now coming to terms with the fact that the Iraqi economy needs to be rebuilt, and the task may require far more financial resources than was needed to oust Saddam from power.

Financial resources for waging the war had been planned for and guaranteed well before the war began. However, the task of reconstructing postwar Iraq was not, and continues not to be, considered with the same determination or tenacity. Of course Iraq has oil and gas, but it would be naïve and highly imprudent to rely on these resources alone for the gigantic project ahead.

While the coalition powers continue to engage the remnants of the insurgents around the Sunni Triangle, the interim Iraqi government has started on the task of economic reconstruction of Iraq. As a matter of fact, the magnitude of financial resources required for this reconstruction exercise has staggered the imagination of many analysts. Are the proceeds from Iraq oil and gas going to be enough? Of course not!

The prewar economic situation of Iraq

The fact that Iraq had endured years of extremely crippling economic sanctions prior to the war makes the reconstruction of its economy a formidable task. The war, the destruction and the looting that followed have further widened the size of the reconstruction exercise required and these, as a result, have raised the magnitude of financial resources required for postwar reconstruction of the economy.

The invasion of Kuwait by Saddam Hussein in 1991 sparked the first Gulf War. The allied forces stopped short of marching to Baghdad, but ensured that Saddam Hussein was no longer able to threaten its neighbours by wiping out his military capability and limiting his economic potential. In effect, substantial parts of Iraqi military and economic infrastructures were severely damaged. As part of the agreement to end the military hostilities, stringent economic and military sanctions were imposed on Baghdad, which were scrupulously enforced. Under the Oil for Food programme that followed, Baghdad was allowed to sell oil abroad under the supervision of an international monitoring group. Only essential medical and consumable items were allowed into Iraq. This went on for more than 10 years, and as a result Iraq witnessed very high levels of inflation, unemployment and negative economic growth.

Twelve years on, and with economic and military sanctions still in place, the second Gulf War was launched in 2003. The destruction of the already devastated economy of Iraq was complete and decisive. In an attempt to hasten the fall of Baghdad, the coalition forces ensured that the transport system, communication networks, and the little remaining production capacity of the Iraqi economy were targeted and destroyed. Then, after the fall of Baghdad, the looting started. Together, these events brought what was left of the state of the Iraqi economy to a complete standstill.

There are estimates from various quarters as to exactly how much would be required for the task of reconstructing the Iraqi economy. In my view, approximately $200 billion may be required. It may be more.

Will earnings from Iraq oil and gas be enough?

Going by its daily output of 2.5 million barrels of crude oil per day, it is unlikely that Iraq will be able to finance such a project from the proceeds of oil and gas alone. Apart from this, it is not possible for Iraq to raise an adequate amount of money at once without having to wait for an unnecessary length of time. The fact that the price of oil remains volatile in the world market makes any forecast of earnings from it a highly risky business. Not only this, the speculative activities of derivative commodity traders on the basis oil and other energy products have the potential of exacerbating the volatility of earnings from oil and gas even further.

Should Iraq approach the IMF or the World Bank? In my view, this is not an option. The reason for this is that these organizations were neither designed nor geared to finance projects of this magnitude. If such moves will be required, they should be optional and should be viewed only as complementary measures to an integrated and highly sophisticated financial package.

While the military operation in Iraq will not be allowed to ground to an inglorious halt due to lack of funds, the economic reconstruction exercise of Iraq could drag on for a decade or even more if financial resources are inadequate and/or untimely. To avoid this, Iraq not only needs an adequate and coherent financial package, it also needs to ensure that such a financial package is delivered within the shortest possible time, to ensure that Iraq reaches its prewar level of development relatively quickly and start experiencing real economic growth.

Nothing short of a well-organized and highly coherent financial package will be sufficient and timely enough to transform Iraq from its present status without undue pain or hardship. This view was reinforced In October 2003 in Madrid where an attempt was made to secure funds for the economic reconstruction of Iraq. Seventy-three donor-countries were in attendance at the fund-raising forum. The aim of the organizers was, among others, to encourage participants to pledge funds to stabilize and reconstruct Iraq. By the time the conference ended, the amount raised was not enough to run Iraq for a month.

This was in spite of efforts by the American Treasury Secretary, John Snow, 'to rally an outpouring of financial support for Iraq' (CNN money, October 2003). Obviously, the nature of the reconstruction task facing Iraq is such that it is beyond the reach of a handful of generous nations reaching deep into their pockets and scoring political points. What is needed is, as mentioned earlier, an integrated and highly coherent financial package to ensure that adequate funds flow into Iraq without placing an undue burden on the economies of donor countries. What package is being proposed, and what is the mechanism for attracting such funds into Iraq? To address these questions, we need, first, to take a brief glance at the economic potential of Iraq.

The economic potential of Iraq

In terms of oil and gas reserves, the economic potential of Iraq is staggering. With over 112 billion barrels of oil reserve, and over 110 trillion cubic feet of proven natural gas (another 150 trillion cubic feet yet untapped), Iraq ranks second in the world after Saudi Arabia (CNN Money, October 2003). The bulk of Iraqi oil and gas deposits are located around the Kirkuk, Ain-Zalah, Butma and Bai Hassan oilfields to the north, and also in the Rumaila and Zubair oilfields to the south.

The annual gross domestic Income of Iraq was estimated to stand at $28.6 billion for the year 2000 (CIA country report on Iraq). At present, Iraq generates about $72 million a day from selling oil in the world market. This equates to about $25billion a year. With the capacity to produce 2.5 million barrels of crude oil per day, it could be argued that Iraq is an extremely rich country by every standard, capable of aspiring to sophisticated socio-economic infrastructure and substantial reserves abroad. Of course, this is dependent on an absence of any major negative volatility in the price of crude oil. In addition to the above-mentioned potentials, Iraq is equally endowed with an army of highly skilled and well-educated workers in their prime age. Contributions of Iraq nationals in the areas of science and technology, research and development and information and communications technology tower above that of any other country from the Middle East with the exception of Israel.

Prior to the second Gulf War, Iraq had suffered tough economic sanctions for more than a decade, and as a result of the war almost all the potentials highlighted above have been wiped out. An unprecedented number of highly skilled and experienced Iraqi nationals moved to seek shelter abroad, and in addition to these factors the huge scale of looting that followed the fall of Baghdad has also contributed to reducing these potentials to almost nothing. In addition, the huge debts facing Iraq and interest payments on these debts are likely to further decimate the real, as opposed to absolute, amount of financial potential available to actually execute any meaningful reconstruction of the Iraqi economy. What then are the options for Iraq?

The case for securitization of Iraqi assets

As a way forward, I am proposing a comprehensive and highly integrated financial leveraging exercise that will give the new Iraq government the much needed financial resources with which to transform Iraq, and make the country itself attractive to its citizens abroad. In specific terms, securitization of Iraq assets is being offered. This will require the new Iraqi government, with support from its creditworthy partners in industrialized societies, to design, standardize, package and then sell a wide variety of financial securities backed by account receivables or future cash flows from its oil and gas to financial institutions around the globe. For investors, this is tantamount to buying a stake in the future cash flow from export earnings of Iraq's oil and gas (Haushalter, 2000).

This approach is different from, and has advantages over, simple exportation of oil and gas from Iraq. The approach would give the Iraqi government an unparalleled and timely access to huge amounts of financial resources from the world's capital markets far beyond the annual receivables from exportation of its oil and gas. This is one of the crucial benefits that the Iraqi government could gain from leveraging its income on the basis of its assets through securitization, as opposed to simply selling the assets abroad for cash. The very size and nature of Iraq's assets make this a credible and highly attractive option for international financial institutions (Haushalter, 2000).

'In a modern and highly sophisticated financial market, there are many things that are close to fulfilling the traditional role of money or capital' (Guyon, 2003). These include highly liquid assets such as share certificates and certificates of deposit, as well as less liquid assets such as credit-card receivables, and oil wells that have potential to generate future earnings or a steady cash flow. By granting investors a legal claim to future earnings from its assets, Iraq could effectively initiate securitization of its assets, and attract institutional and private investors from around the world.

A famous and highly successful musician (David Bowie) once raised $55 million from the international financial markets. All he needed as a security was evidence of future earnings from his music – his royalty (Guyon, 2003). By issuing commercial papers, secured against its oil reserve or potential earning from its assets, Iraq could effectively securitize its assets and tap in to funds available from the international capital markets. With such a huge amount of potential future earnings from its assets, Iraq would be well-positioned to enjoy three distinct and fortuitously timed benefits. Firstly, Iraq would be able to raise enormous amounts of money from the world financial markets well above its estimated annual income from the same oil and gas reserves combined together. Secondly, Iraq would be immune from the volatility of oil prices. And thirdly, Iraq could have access to such financial resources at a time when they are most needed without having to wait.

The very fact that such financial products are tradable in secondary markets across the world provides the much-needed depth for the market as this ensures liquidity for financial products. This, in turn, renders the products more attractive to investors and further enhances their market value (Severn, 1974).

The process of securitization requires certain steps to be undertaken. These include, first of all, forming a group of originators that will design, evaluate and create oil and gas-income receivables for Iraq. This role could be fulfilled by private institutions such as Morgan Stanley, Merrill Lynch or other financial intermediaries of high reputation. The next step is the process of pooling and standardization of the fragmented investment package, necessary to structure the investment programme in a manner that suits the needs and profiles of a variety of institutional investors (Chance, 2004).

The next stage in the asset securitization process is the credit-enhancement exercise. Usually, this can be done for a fee by a coalition of highly reputable and well-rated financial organizations. Together with the standardization exercise, the credit-enhancement exercise facilitates the marketability of such financial securities and enhances their market value. A well-standardized and credit-enhanced financial instrument will command the attention of worldwide investors. This extremely crucial exercise will be explored in detail later.

The next stage in the securitization process is to set up a special-purpose vehicle or mechanism created solely to organize, standardize, evaluate and then issue the asset-backed Iraq securities to investors. Pooling of income receivables from the sale of Iraqi assets is similar to creating a pool of credit-card debtors in another form of asset-backed securities, or, as another example, mortgage-backed securitization. The huge demand for crude oil in the international market arena also makes the sector more attractive to investors (Haushalter, 2000; Bodie, 2005).

Securitization of Iraq's assets: the prerequisites

In order for such a securitization exercise to be successful, a number of conditions or prerequisites must be met to facilitate the process and make Iraq attractive to international investors. The extent to which these conditions are met will determine how the international financial community views the new postwar Iraq.

Prominent among these prerequisites is the need to pacify the former Iraq creditors who had lent huge amount of money to the Saddam regime secured against future revenues from Iraqi oil. Unless Iraq settles or reaches an agreement on its outstanding debts, it is unlikely that it will be rated highly in the international capital markets. In this category of creditors are China, Russia and France. These are permanent members of the United Nations Security Council, and they command substantial influence both economically and politically in the international capital arena (Guyon, 2003).

One possible way of addressing this particular problem is to ask for a debt-relief package for Iraq. Faced with unprecedented demand for crude oil to fuel its rapid economic growth, China is most likely to support this move. Russia and France could then be offered a reasonable stake in a future economic reconstruction programme of Iraq in exchange for their support. According to International Monetary Fund estimates, Iraq owed over $120 billion to its creditors as at 2003. If about 80 per cent of this figure were written off or forgiven, this might clear the way for addressing other prerequisites.

Foremost among these other prerequisites is the creation of enforceable financial regulations and a general rule of law in Iraq. Institutional and private investors as well as other organizations, which might be interested in having a commercial relationship with Iraq, will undoubtedly be motivated if this condition is met. It is not yet clear whether the new Iraq will embrace the international rule of law or embrace Islamic law based on Sharia doctrines. The new Iraq stands to attract substantial amounts of foreign capital and expatriates via asset-securitization if it modifies the existing Sharia law to accommodate the concerns of foreign investors, or leave religion out of business altogether. In view of its position amongst Islamic states, and non-pluralism in its present socio-cultural inclination, the prospect of Iraq being a secular state is not plausible, at least for now. Next on the list of prerequisites for the securitization of Iraq's assets is the need to have a reliable social, economic and physical infrastructure in Iraq. On this list are: good transport systems, uninterrupted power supplies, reliable telecommunications, highly efficient public-service centres – including a national economic information department, immigration office and national health service (Rawls, 1995).

In order to have a successful securitization of its assets with substantial participation of foreign organizations, it is equally imperative that the new Iraq regime pursues a transparent and highly coherent fiscal and monetary policy, which could be perceived as healthy and prudent by potential foreign partners. These include, but are not limited to, a stable and favourable exchange rate of the new Iraq dina, a manageable level of inflation and unemployment, and a permissible volume of external debts (Erb, 1995).

Equally important is the stability of the future political and social system of Iraq. It is estimated that thousands of foreign fighters who are fiercely loyal to al-Qaeda have teamed-up with local Iraqi insurgents. As a result, the spate of kidnapping and killing of foreign nationals in Iraq has gone beyond an alarming stage. This is without considering the dozens of innocent Iraqi civilians who are being massacred almost on a daily basis. For now (at the time of writing, in July 2005), the interim government of Iraq appears powerless to maintain law and order or to create an environment stable enough to attract foreign investors. To improve the situation, more military assistance will undoubtedly be needed from the coalition allies in order to ensure a violence-free and politically stable Iraq.

Yet another coalition?

In order to achieve the task of military invasion of Iraq, a coalition of a multinational forces was put together, that ensured that the burden, most notably military hardware and personnel, was shared among coalition members. America alone contributes a far greater proportion, from all perspectives, than any other member of the military coalition.

To ensure a quick and smooth flow of international capital to Iraq, it is extremely important that the key Iraq allies (including America, Britain, Australia, Japan and selected members of the G-8 countries) form yet another coalition to underwrite some of the capital shift to Iraq. This is a crucial aspect of the securitization process. It can be construed to mean offering a credit-enhancement opportunity to the new Iraq government, and essentially involves third parties – in this case the G-8 and other influential coalition member countries – offering guarantee to investors regarding the creditworthiness of the new Iraq, and timely payment of its contractual obligations (Fabozzi, 1994; Sundaresan, 2002).

Under normal circumstances, this could be arranged with a syndicate of top-grade financial intermediaries for a substantial fee. This exercise would have the potential of transforming the risk assessment of Iraq to a permissible level for international investors. Such a credit-enhancement exercise would encourage a wide variety of institutional investors who, otherwise, might be forbidden from participating due to the Basle-II protocol on risk exposure and management.

The significance of this exercise cannot be overemphasized. It will enable commercial papers issued by Baghdad, to which the enhancement exercise applies, to be given an investment-grade rating far above that of the state of Iraq itself. This will make the new Iraq commercially attractive to investors around the globe (Fabozzi, 1993). Underwriting countries are likely to lose nothing from guaranteeing loans to, or investment in, Iraq. These coalition states could, in turn, hedge or effectively limit their exposures in standing as guarantors for Iraq by making specific arrangements for Iraqi oil revenue to be paid into an escrow account outside the country, where such proceeds would be available to creditors who buy the oil-backed financial securities from the new regime in Baghdad (Fabozzi, 1994; Bodie, 2005).

The United States of America has made similar arrangements before. After the fall of communism in Russia, the American Export-Import Bank created similar financial arrangements for the Russian oil and gas industry. The effect of this was a massive influx of capital into Russia's energy sector from the industrialized countries (Guyon, 2003). Similar arrangements were also made in the mid-1990s by the New York Federal Reserve to help finance the oil industry in Mexico.

If there is a genuine will to reconstruct Iraq, securitization of its assets on the basis of credit enhancement by highly credible coalition states is feasible, commercially prudent and less risky, and definitely not beyond reach.

One distinctive benefit that this credit-enhancement exercise might bring to Iraqi investors is that it would enable them to better quantify and eventually manage their exposures in Iraq. Apart from this, the credit-enhancement opportunity might enable corporate entities in Iraq to benefit from raising capital from abroad as well.

Sources of finance open to Iraq

A list of financial sources open to Iraq includes, but is not limited to, the following:

- international fixed-income markets (sovereign, regional and corporate);
- international equity markets;
- syndicated international loans;
- global venture-capital markets;
- international derivatives markets (hedge funds and fund of funds);
- the International Bank for Reconstruction and Development;
- the International Monetary Fund;
- the International Financial Corporation;
- bilateral financial arrangements;
- Iraqi wholesale banks abroad;
- internal savings and deposits of Iraqis;
- income from oil and gas exploration licences;
- privatization of state-owned corporations;
- selling of Iraq oil abroad; and
- counterparties structured notes.

The majority of these financial sources requires the prerequisites mentioned earlier to be satisfactorily met.

The issue of risk

Risk must not be overlooked; major financial centres around the world are keen to adopt a common policy in terms of appraisal and management of their risks. Within the Basel-II agreement, any form of ambiguities, inconsistencies and non-uniformity in the way and manner in which financial exposures are administered and managed are being scrutinized and augmented by financial authorities and institutions around the world. Iraq stands to improve its credit rating before the world financial community if it embraces and adheres to recommendations of the Basel-II agreement (Dallas, 1993; Dubovsky, 2003).

An investor who contemplates venturing into Iraq is likely to be faced with a variety of risks, including exchange-rate volatility, the volatility of Iraqi future receivables, the huge amount of external debt, as well as corruption and mismanagement of the national economy of the new Iraq. Other forms of risk that foreign investors might face include: the prospect of nationalization of foreign commercial interests; indigenization of foreign commercial ventures; debt default or renegotiation; and the possibility of civil disorder and the risk of religious extremism (Buckley, 2004; Bodie, 2005). By addressing most of the prerequisites discussed above, it is very likely that the new Iraqi government would be able to minimize or even eliminate some of these risks.

Quantitative risk management

It is not enough to enumerate the various types of risks a potential investor is likely to encounter by including Iraq in his/her portfolio; it is equally necessary to suggest ways of quantifying and managing those risks. In this regard, ratio analysis, and discounted cash-flow methods appear to be very appropriate.

Of all the risks that a potential investor in an asset-backed security is likely to face, the threat of changes in the price of a security due to changes in interest rates in the market occupies a unique position. A rise in interest rates will lead to a fall in the price of any fixed-income or debt security. Conversely, a fall in the interest rate will trigger an increase in prices of such securities. As a result, the interest rate is considered to be one of the major determinants of price of fixed income or asset-backed security.

By applying integral calculus to a price–yield equation of a fixed-income security, it is possible to ascertain by how much the price of such a security will change if the rates of interest change by just one unit. To show this, a price–yield equation for a fixed-income security needs to be presented first. Given that the yield of an asset-backed security being proposed for Iraq is paid semi-annually, the price–yield relationship of such an instrument, provided it is default-free and has N number of yields left, can be written as:

$$P = \frac{\frac{C}{2}}{\left(1 + \frac{Y}{2}\right)} + \frac{\frac{C}{2}}{\left(1 + \frac{Y}{2}\right)^2} + \frac{\frac{C}{2}}{\left(1 + \frac{Y}{2}\right)^3} + \cdots\cdots\cdots + \frac{\frac{C}{2} + 100}{\left(1 + \frac{Y}{2}\right)^N}$$

(8.1)

where $C/2$ represents the semi-annual coupon, Y the yield, and N the number of years remaining before maturity. It is assumed that the security is offered at $100 each at par.

Using summation notation, this equation can be transformed into:

$$P = \sum_{j=1}^{N} \frac{\frac{C}{2}}{\left(1 + \frac{Y}{2}\right)^j} + \frac{100}{\left(1 + \frac{Y}{2}\right)^n}$$

(8.2)

where the first term, with the summation sign, represents the present value of all future semi-annual returns, and the second term indicates the present value of the balloon payment on the security.

A more simple analytical relationship between the price of a fixed-income security, which has exactly N rounds of yield payments that matures in $N/2$ years, and its semi-annually compounded yield can be specified thus:

$$P = \frac{C}{Y} + \frac{100 - \frac{C}{Y}}{\left(1 + \frac{Y}{2}\right)^N}$$

(8.3)

Applying the concept of differential calculus, it is possible to find the $\partial P/\partial Y$ of equation (8.3). This will enable us to determine any fluctuation in the price of the security as its interest rate changes by one unit. This is equivalent to determining the price risk (or interest-rate risk) of an asset-backed security similar to the one being proposed for Iraq.

Denoting this risk as a measure of change in the price of the security in terms of change in its yield, it is possible to postulate that:

$$-\frac{\partial P}{\partial Y} = \frac{C}{Y^2}\left(1 - \frac{1}{\left(1 + \frac{Y}{2}\right)^n}\right) + \frac{N\left(100 - \frac{C}{Y}\right)}{2\left(1 + \frac{Y}{2}\right)^{N+1}} \tag{8.4}$$

where N represents the number of coupons remaining to be settled, and Y the yield on the security. This equation can be modified to determine the interest-rate risk or price risk of similar fixed-income securities such as gilt edge or treasury bonds (Sundaresan, 2002). The negative sign in $-(\partial P/\partial Y)$ denotes the inverse relationship between price and yield.

As a matter of fact, the price of a fixed income security tends to be more volatile with respect to a change in interest rates the longer the term to maturity of the security. It is unlikely that the new Iraqi regime will be able to start to meet its huge financial obligations emanating from this securitization process almost immediately and, as a result, might want to opt for some 'quiet period' before starting to pay returns. This will make lengthening the term of the security more preferable to Baghdad even though this is likely to drive-up the price of such a financial instrument. The prospect of this makes interest-rate risk (or price risk) almost inevitable for investors in the Iraqi security.

It is possible to scale this price risk by a factor of 100 in order to reflect a change in price for a percentage change in yield:

$$-\frac{\frac{\partial P}{\partial Y}}{100} = \frac{1}{100}\left(\frac{C}{Y^2}\left(1 - \frac{1}{\left(1 + \frac{Y}{2}\right)^N}\right) + \frac{N\left(100 - \frac{C}{Y}\right)}{2\left(1 + \frac{Y}{2}\right)^{N+1}}\right) \tag{8.5}$$

The most effective way of hedging or managing any Iraqi exposures would undoubtedly extend beyond being prudent in trading in fundamental financial products alone and applying quantitative methods to quantify the magnitude of risk involved. Consideration must be given to applying sophisticated derivative financial products specifically designed for hedging, managing and, where appropriate, speculating on risks (Hughes, 1975; Fabozzi, 1994).

These derivative products could be equity-based derivatives (including stocks, bonds, interest rates and commodities). Other forms could be structured notes as well as exotic derivatives. Apart from being fundamentally different, they all have one thing in common – that is, application of options, futures, swaps and swaptions to speculate and/or manage future prices of a range of underlying financial assets (Chance, 2004; Hull, 2003; Kolb, 2003).

Qualitative risk management

Another approach to managing risk or exposure in Iraq would be for individual investors to negotiate mutually acceptable conditions with the new Iraqi regime. Depending on the size, nature of investment and the sector of the Iraq economy being targeted, individual investors who apply early enough are likely to get some special privileges (Lessard, 1976).

Such bilateral arrangements must not seek to replace the need to meet the prerequisites already mentioned above; but rather serve the purpose of complementing other risk-managing efforts being considered. 'There is no universal, clear-cut response to the issue of exposure management. Different firms will adopt different postures because their varying degrees of risk aversion, and also because their exposures will vary from time to time' (Buckley, 2004).

References

Abdullah, F.A. (1987) *Financial Management for the Multinational Firm* (Englewood Cliffs, New Jersey: Prentice-Hall).
Aliber, R.Z. (1979) *Exchange Risk and Corporate International Finance* (New York: Wiley).
Artis, M. and Taylor, M.P. (1990) 'International Financial Stability and the Regulation of Capital Flows', in G. Bird (ed.), *The International Financial Regime* (Guildford: University of Surrey Press).
Barnett, G. and Rosenberg, M. (1983) *International Diversification in Bonds*, Prudential International Fixed Income Investment Strategy, vol. 2.
Berkman, H. and Bradbury, M.E. (1996) 'Empirical Evidence on the Corporate Use of Derivatives', *Financial Management* (Summer), vol. 25, pp. 5–13.
Bodie, Z., Kane, A. and Marcus, A.J. (2005) *Investments* (New York: McGraw-Hill).
Buckley, A. (2004) *Multinational Finance*, 5th edn (Harlow: Prentice-Hall).
Buckley, A., Buckley, P., Langevin, P. and Tse, K. (1996) 'The Financial Analysis of Foreign Investment Decisions by Large UK-based Companies', *European Journal of Finance*, vol. 2(2), pp. 181–206.

Business International (1979) 'Policies of Multinational Corporations on Debt/Equity Mix', *Money Report*, vol. 21 (September), pp. 319–20.

Cantor, R. and Packer, F. (1994) 'The Credit Rating Industry', *Federal Reserve Bank of New York Quarterly Review*, vol. 19(2), pp. 1–26.

Chance, D.M. (2004) *An Introduction to Derivatives and Risk Management*, (Ohio: Thompson Learning). Mason, Ohio, Australia.

CNN Money News series (24 October 2003), Snow, J.: Iraq Pledges Gaining Momentum, news series 24 October 2003.

Collier, P.A. and Davis, E.W. (1985) 'Currency Risk Management in UK Multinational Companies', *Accounting and Business Research* (Autumn), pp. 327–35.

Dallas, G. (1990) 'A Rating Agency View', *The Treasurer* (July–August), pp. 26–7.

Dubovsky, D.A. and Miller Jr, T.W. (2003) *Derivatives: Valuation and Risk Management* (New York: Oxford University Press).

Dunn, K. and MacConnell, J.J. (1981) 'Valuation of GNMA Mortgage-backed Securities', *Journal of Finance*, vol. 36(3), pp. 599–616.

Erb, C.B., Harvey, C.R. and Viskanta, T.E. (1995) 'Country Risk and Global Equity Selection', *Journal of Portfolio Management*, vol. 21(2), pp. 74–83.

Fabozzi, F. (1993) *Bond Markets, Analysis and Strategies* (Englewood Cliffs, New Jersey: Prentice-Hall).

Fabozzi, F. (ed.) (1994) *Handbook of Fixed Income Securities* (Homewood, Illinois: Irwin).

French, K.R. and Poterba, J.M. (1991) 'Investor Diversification and International Equity Markets', *American Economic Review*, vol. 81, pp. 222–6.

Geczy, C., Minton, B.A. and Schrand, C. (1997) 'Why Firms Use Currency Derivatives', *Journal of Finance*, vol. 52, pp. 1323–54.

Guyon, J. (2003) *Fortune*, vol. 15, August edition, p. 15.

Haushalter, G.D. (2000) 'Financing Policy, Basis Risk and Corporate Hedging: Evidence from Oil and Gas Producers', *Journal of Finance*, vol. 55, pp. 107–52.

Hughes, J.S., Logue, D.E. and Sweeney, R.J. (1975) 'Corporate International Diversification and Market Assigned Measures of Risk and Diversification', *Journal of Finance and Quantitative Analysis*, vol. 10(4), pp. 627–37.

Hull, J.C. (2003) *Options, Futures, and Other Derivatives* (New Jersey: Prentice-Hall).

Hunter, J.E. and Coggin, T.D. (1990) 'An Analysis of the Diversification Benefit from International Equity Investment', *Journal of Portfolio Management*, vol. 17(1), pp. 33–6.

Jacque, L. and Hawawini, G. (1993) 'Myths and Realities of the Global Capital Market: Lessons for Financial Managers', *Journal of Applied Corporate Finance*, vol. 6(3), pp. 81–90.

Kolb, R.W. (2003) *Futures, Options, and Swaps* (Oxford: Blackwell).

Lessard, D.R. (1996) 'Incorporating Country Risk in the Valuation of Offshore Projects', *Journal of Applied Corporate Finance*, vol. 9(3), pp. 52–63.

Rawls III, S.W. and Smithson, C.W. (1990) 'Strategic Risk Management', *Journal of Applied Corporate Finance*, vol. 2(4), pp. 6–18.

Ray, C. (1993) *The Bond Market, Trading and Risk Management* (Homewood, Illinois: Irwin).

Severn, A.K. (1974) 'Investor Evaluation of Foreign and Domestic Risk', *Journal of Finance*, vol. 29, pp. 545–50.

Shapiro, A.C. and Rutenberg, D.P. (1976) 'Managing Exchange Risks in a Floating World', *Financial Management* (Summer), pp. 48–58.

Sundaresan, S.M. (2002) *Fixed Income Markets and their Derivatives* (London: Thompson Learning).

United Nations (1993) *World Investment Report* of the Transnational Corporations and Management Division of the United Nations (Geneva: UN).

Wang, W. (1995) 'Analysis of Mortgage-backed Securities', unpublished PhD dissertation, Columbia University.

Wilson, M. (1990) 'Empirical Evidence of the Use of a Framework of Risk and Return in Capital Budgeting for Foreign Direct Investment', *Managerial Finance*, vol. 16(2), pp. 25–34.

Index